Understanding
JEAN-PAUL SARTRE

UNDERSTANDING MODERN EUROPEAN and LATIN AMERICAN LITERATURE

JAMES HARDIN, *SERIES EDITOR*

ADVISORY BOARD

* * * * *

Understanding Günter Grass
by Alan Frank Keele

Understanding Samuel Beckett
by Alan Astro

Understanding Graciliano Ramos
by Celso Lemos de Oliveira

Understanding Jean-Paul Sartre
by Philip R. Wood

Understanding Gabriel García Márquez
by Kathleen McNerney

Understanding Albert Camus
by David R. Ellison

Understanding Claude Simon
by Ralph Sarkonak

Understanding Max Frisch
by Wulf Koepke

Understanding Mario Vargas Llosa
by Sara Castro-Klarén

UNDERSTANDING

JEAN-PAUL SARTRE

By PHILIP R. WOOD

UNIVERSITY OF SOUTH CAROLINA PRESS

Published in Columbia, South Carolina, by the
University of South Carolina Press

Manufactured in the United States of America

First Edition

Library of Congress Cataloging-in-Publication Data

Wood, Philip R.
  Understanding Jean-Paul Sartre / by Philip R. Wood.—1st ed.
    p.   cm.—(Understanding modern European and Latin
American literature)
  Includes bibliographical references and index.
  ISBN 0-87249-703-8
  1. Sartre, Jean Paul, 1905– —Criticism and interpretation.
I. Title. II. Series.
PQ2637.A82Z97   1990
848'.91409—dc20   90-37954

CONTENTS

EDITOR'S PREFACE

Understanding Modern European and Latin American Literature has been planned as a series of guides for undergraduate and graduate students and nonacademic readers. Like its companion series, *Understanding Contemporary American Literature,* the aim of the books is to provide an introduction to the life and writings of prominent modern authors and to explicate their most important works.

Modern literature makes special demands, and this is particularly true of foreign literature, in which the reader must contend not only with unfamiliar, often arcane artistic conventions and philosophical concepts, but also with the handicap of reading the literature in translation. It is a truism that the nuances of one language can be rendered in another only imperfectly (and this problem is especially acute in fiction), but the fact that the works of European and Latin American writers are situated in a historical and cultural setting quite different from our own can be as great a hindrance to the understanding of these works as the linguistic barrier. For this reason, the UMELL series emphasizes the sociological and historical background of the writers treated. The peculiar philosophical and cultural traditions of a given culture may be particularly important for an understanding of certain authors, and these will be taken up in the introductory chapter and also in the discussion of those works to which this information is relevant. Beyond this, the books will treat the specifically literary aspects of the author under discussion and attempt to explain the complexities of contemporary literature lucidly. The books are conceived as introductions to the authors covered, not as comprehensive analyses. They do not provide detailed summaries of plot since they are meant to be used in conjunction with the books they treat, not as a substitute for the study of the original works. It is our hope that the UMELL series will help to increase knowledge and understanding of the European and Latin American cultures and will serve to make the literature of those cultures more accessible.

Professor Wood's *Understanding Jean-Paul Sartre* fills the need for an up-to-date, comprehensive study in English. It stresses the fact that Sartre's writings were a response to historical trends dating back to the simultaneous birth of modernity and capitalism in the West at the end of the Middle Ages. These trends, with the subsequent spread of a market economy into all walks of life, would eventually culminate in Nietzsche's "death of God" and the novel theme of the absurdity of existence now indissolubly associated with Sartre's name. Wood links Sartre's other major themes—existential freedom, socialist revolution, alienation, authenticity, and death—with these factors as well as less obvious ones such as the nuclear family of modernity and modern gender ideology. I believe that the book succeeds in making comprehensible the broad outlines of Sartre's complex oeuvre in large part because of its close attention to the historic data.

J.H.

In accordance with the aims of the series of which it is a part, this book attempts to make those of Sartre's literary works which are most frequently read more accessible to students and the general public.

I have tried to achieve this end while confronting most of the important and difficult questions which any major writer's work—and Sartre's in particular— gives rise to in readers both within and outside the academy. To this extent I would hope that this book will serve as more than a mere introduction. I have, however, striven not to assume any prior background in philosophy, psychoanalysis, Marxism, feminism or literary critical theory. As a consequence, some readers will necessarily find some of the explanations a bit labored. But I would like to think that no allowances have been made in terms of the size or relevance of the questions engaged with.

There may be some surprise at the omission of any treatment of Sartre's autobiographical volume, *Words*. It has seemed to me that an account of this work— within the critical perspective which interests me— would have entailed the kind of full-length examination which would have exceeded the limits of this study.

English translations of the original French are my own. I have nonetheless borrowed gratefully from the published translations of Lloyd Alexander, Gerard

Hopkins, Eric Sutton, and others. All page references, however, are to the English translations cited in the bibliography.

ABBREVIATIONS

1905	Jean-Paul Sartre is born in Paris, 21 June.
1906	Father dies. Lives henceforth with mother and grandparents.
1917	Mother remarries. The family moves to La Rochelle.
1920	Returns to Paris.
1921/22	Baccalauréat.
1924–29	Ecole Normale Supérieure.
1928	Fails the national *agrégation* examination in philosophy through trying to be too original.
1929	Meets Simone de Beauvoir. They become lovers and make a pact to remain together for the rest of their lives while each remaining free to engage in other relationships. Passes *agrégation* in first place after having decided to conform to conventional expectations. Simone de Beauvoir is in second place in the same examination.
1929–31	Military service.
1931	Starts career as a schoolteacher of philosophy (which he will abandon when fame makes it financially possible to do so after the Second World War).
1938	Publishes *Nausea*.
1939	Conscripted.
1940	Prisoner of war.
1941	Escapes.

1941–43　Helps found a Resistance group which soon collapses; writes for the underground *Lettres françaises*.

1943　Publishes *The Flies* and *Being and Nothingness*.

1945　Publishes *No Exit, The Age of Reason, The Reprieve*. Turns down Legion of Honor.

1948　Publishes *Dirty Hands*.

1949　Publishes *Troubled Sleep*.

1950　Denounces Soviet concentration camps.

1951　Publishes *The Devil and the Good Lord*.

1952　First positive relations with the French Communist Party (having been frequently denounced by the party up to this point). Writes *The Communists and Peace*—probably the work which brought him closest to the Communist Party, despite significant differences, in which, despite severe reservations about the Soviet Union, he took their side in the Cold War, seeing the United States as the principal aggressor. This work has been held against Sartre ever since. Despite his subsequent denunciations of the Communist Party and the Soviet Union, Sartre will refuse ever to repudiate this essay, believing it was right in the context of the time. Publishes *Saint Genet*.

1954　Writes enthusiastically about a trip to the Soviet Union. Is made vice-president of the France–USSR Association. Spends two months in the People's Republic of China.

1956　Votes for the local communist candidate in national elections. In November denounces the Soviet invasion of Hungary and severs relations with the French Communist Party. Takes first of many initiatives against French government policies (torture, massacre of civilians) in the Algerian war of independence.

1960–66 Numerous visits to the Soviet Union. Meets Khrushchev. Visits Cuba, meets with Castro and Che Guevara.

1960 Publishes *The Condemned of Altona* and *Critique of Dialectical Reason*.

1962 Apartment severely damaged by bomb planted by right-wing extremists in favor of a continued French colonial presence in Algeria.

1963 Publishes the autobiographical *Words*.

1964 Is awarded the Nobel Prize for literature. Turns it down, not wishing, among other reasons, to become "an institution."

1965 Cancels plans to lecture at Cornell University as protest against the Vietnam war.

1966 Accepts Bertrand Russell's invitation to participate in a tribunal investigating American war crimes in Vietnam.

1967 Declines to take part in the Tenth Congress of Soviet Writers in order to protest the trial of the dissident writers Sinyavsky and Daniel. Visits both Israel and Egypt. Defends the right to exist of both Israel and a Palestinian state.

1968 Openly supports the May insurrection in Paris. Accuses the French Communist Party of having sold the insurrection down the

river. Condemns the Soviet invasion of
Czechoslovakia.

1969   Protests the expulsion of Solzhenitsyn from
the Union of Soviet Writers.

1970   Assumes the editorship of the extreme left-
wing *La Cause du peuple,* after previous two
editors have been imprisoned.

1971   Severs relations with Castro over the im-
prisonment of Padilla. Publishes first two
volumes of vast biographical study of
Flaubert, *The Family Idiot.*

1973   Onset of incurable semiblindness. Can no
longer read or write. Supports Israel in the
Yom Kippur war.

1974   Visits the German terrorist Andreas Baader
in prison and protests his conditions of im-
prisonment. Declares, however, that terrorism, while valid in Latin America, is a political error in Western Europe.

1976   Film *Sartre by Himself,* a series of interviews, appears in Paris cinemas.

1980   Supports boycott of the Moscow Olympic
Games in protest over the invasion of Afghanistan. Dies, 15 April, intestate and
heavily in debt to his publishers, having
spent the fortune he had earned as a celebrated writer on friends, women, travel, acts
of personal charity, and innumerable political causes. A crowd of fifty thousand people
forms his funeral cortege. In conformity
with his wishes, his remains are buried
without ceremony or speeches.

Understanding
JEAN-PAUL SARTRE

CHAPTER ONE

Introduction

A. "One does not arrest Voltaire"; "Shoot Sartre!"[1]

Had Jean-Paul Sartre written only his plays or his novels, or had he written only his enormous philosophical treatises like *Being and Nothingness* and the *Critique of Dialectical Reason,* or had he even limited himself to the role of the polemical essayist of the *Situations* volumes, his reputation would have been assured. As it is, the sheer range and volume of his work is astonishing by any standards. In twentieth-century Western philosophy there have been only two other figures who have enjoyed an acclaim comparable to that achieved by Sartre: Heidegger and Wittgenstein; and only these two writers can lay claim to a comparable degree of influence on the course of recent European philosophy, despite the neglect, and denigration even, which Sartre's work has suffered at the hands of the generation of philosophers who have succeeded him in France since the mid-1960s.

It is also true that no other writer or philosopher has been vilified to the same extent as Sartre. For example, at the height of his fame and notoriety the public opposition he displayed toward the brutal suppression by the French government of the Algerian people's insurrection against their colonial occupiers was the cause of his apartment being blown up by right-wing extremists. In this period *Paris-Match* described Sartre as "this civil war machine."

At the same time Sartre aroused intense enthusiasm and loyalty in people: probably no other writer or philosopher has ever dominated French thought as completely and massively as he did between the end of the Second World War and the early 60s. Even though by the time he died in 1980 his reputation had declined considerably, as a cluster of younger writers took over his place at the center of French philosophy, his funeral cortege, some fifty thousand people, has had no rival as an expression of popular loyalty and respect since the death of Victor Hugo a hundred years before. Not even Heidegger and Wittgenstein were ever accorded worldwide public attention to the same extent as Sartre was.

That such passions could be aroused by a mere writer appears strange in the Anglo-Saxon world where it would be inconceivable for a representative of "high" culture to be taken this seriously or accorded this much attention (favorable or otherwise). The differences between France and the United States in this respect are demonstrated by the fact that in the Vietnam war—a war which had as divisive an effect on America as the Algerian war of independence did on France—the public figure who most resembled Sartre in earning for herself the undying hatred of the supporters of the American war effort was not an eminent writer but someone who was, at the time, primarily perceived as a Hollywood sex symbol, Jane Fonda. (This is no reflection on Ms Fonda, who is, of course, a good deal more than this.)

There are a number of reasons for this major difference between the two countries. One reason is that many of the most distinctive products of what we think of as "French culture"—that with which foreigners tend to identify the French, and that with which they proudly identify themselves—have been the product of older forms of economic production (originally artesanal) than those which prevail in the world of today; thus, *haute coûture,* wine and *cuisine.* Alternatively—as in the case of the French language itself, architecture (Versailles, for example), or literature—French culture has frequently existed, in a more or less conflictual way, as an instrument of the originally monarchic French state, national prestige, and power. To this day the French, on the whole, tend to identify themselves with a culture which—despite its considerable achievements in modern technology and so on—is heavily marked by its premodern, preindustrial characteristics. This is often reflected in the attitude of the French toward the United States—an attitude in which envy, scorn, emulation, and sour grapes frequently coexist. To the extent that the United States is commonly identified (both by Americans and by foreigners) as primarily a demotic mass culture of which the characteristic cultural products are high technology, the mass-produced industrial commodity, the mass-cultural television series (*Dallas*), or the mass-cultural entertainer (Michael Jackson)—rather than as the culture of, say, the novels of Melville and Faulkner—the converse valorization of national "high" culture has been one of the means whereby France has tried to compensate its decline from the status of a world power it enjoyed for over two centuries to that of a second-order one.

In order to understand not only the intensity of the reaction to Sartre but also the extremely aggressive, querulous, and sometimes oracular tenor of his writings, it is essential to bear in mind this extraordinary importance accorded "high" culture in France, an importance immensely greater than that enjoyed by its equivalent forms not only in America but even in much of the rest of Europe.

B. The Writer in France and the French State

One crucial reason for this importance accorded high culture, and literature in particular—which may initially seem a rather remote cause and which will oblige us to make a brief detour here through French history—is that a stable centralized modern state, as we recognize it today in the West, emerged more than a century later in France than, for example, in England, France's great rival for world domination in the eighteenth and nineteenth centuries. The thoroughness and ruthlessness of the Norman conquest of England (a relatively small and easily administered territory anyway) meant that even in the Middle Ages the monarchy already enjoyed a measure of authority and administrative control without a rival throughout Western Europe.[2] Even the War of the Roses was more a struggle for control of this centralized state apparatus than the kind of challenge to the centralizing state itself that characterized such aristocratic revolts of the French nobility as the *Fronde* of the seventeenth century. To this day France remains Europe's largest country, and the territory over which the medieval French kings sought—amidst frequent failure—to as-

4

sert their expanding authority was several times more populous than England and also linguistically more diverse. France only emerged with a stable absolutist state to compare with that of Henry VIII in the England of the early sixteenth century more than a hundred years later, after the *Fronde*. In the meantime the three terrible crises of dismemberment and chaos unleashed by the Hundred Years War in the fifteenth century, the religious wars of the sixteenth century, and the *Fronde* left the French monarchy with a built-in need for absolutism and central state control which would reach its apotheosis with Louis XIV, and continues to mark French political life to this day.

It is hard to exaggerate the importance of this turbulent national history as an origin of that unusually high prestige accorded literature in France which is so alien to the American reader and therefore risks standing in the way of understanding. Without literature's being granted this status, Sartre's career as an extraordinarily aggressive literary polemicist (itself alien to an American or British reading public, for reasons to be explained subsequently) would have been impossible. For example, in the construction of the central state power every instrument at hand was grasped: in 1634, in a move which again seems very strange to political practice in the West today, probably the greatest architect of the modern French state, Louis XIII's great minister, Cardinal Richelieu, founded the *Académie française*. Section 26 of the statutes of the academy pledged to produce a dictionary (which was done in due course), a grammar, and a rhetoric of the French language (which never appeared). Section 24 of the statutes declared that "the principal function of the Academy shall be to work with all the care and all the diligence possible to give definite rules to our language, and to render it pure, eloquent, and capable of treating the arts and sciences."[3] This was a deliberate attempt to exert royal central control over the literary and linguistic destiny of the country by imposing upon it a uniform style and ideological tenor that would enhance the country's precarious unity. (As Napoleon would put it a couple of centuries later, you can do anything with a bayonet except sit on it; that is, for a society not to exist in a state of permanent civil war, it is necessary that its members, especially those at the bottom of the pile, accept that the prevailing dispensation of power and privilege is legitimate. One needs, in other words, to integrate the population *ideologically* into a social order.) One mark of the success of Richelieu's operation is that the sixteenth-century writer Rabelais is considerably less accessible, linguistically, to the French today than the seventeenth-century Corneille (an exact contemporary of the founding of the academy), despite the fact that only one century separates the two writers.

The consequences of the creation of the *Académie* for the subsequent literary history of the country have been considerable. It immediately made it plain, for example (something which could be more easily forgotten elsewhere), that literature is always *a political act*. Within two years of its foundation the *Académie* was already being sharply critical of Corneille's great masterpiece *Le Cid* because (among other reasons) of its sympathetic portrayal of dueling, which had recently been outlawed by Richelieu as one of his many attempts to exert state control over the militarized nobility. This kind of historical presence of the state in the country's cultural institutions has meant that literature, like everything else in France, is instantly perceived in its political dimension and judged accordingly in a way that is only found elsewhere today with comparable intensity in Soviet Russia. This attempt to bring literature under the aegis of the state and make it serve the state is not, furthermore, something of the past; thus it is still customary today for great French writers to have state funerals. Typically, Sartre refused to have one. This did not, however, prevent the French president, Giscard d'Estaing (a man who stands for everything Sartre loathed and spent his life combating, and who can in no sense be said to be a sincere admirer of Sartre), from attempting to get some political mileage out of Sartre's death by declaring that Sartre had influenced him in his youth and insisting on spending an hour in respectful vigil over the body. It has also been customary for French presidents to surround themselves with well-known writers and thinkers in an attempt to annex something of their prestige; thus, in our own time General de Gaulle made André Malraux his Minister of Cultural Affairs, and President Mitterand has placed men like Jacques Attali and Régis Debray among his advisers. This custom dates from the monarchy's similarly motivated patronage of the arts; and indeed, as has often been remarked, the French republican presidency remains very monarchic in its style. For example, if one examines almost any photograph of de Gaulle, Pompidou, Giscard d'Estaing, or even the socialist Mitterand with a foreign head of state (especially the British mon-

arch!—nearly a thousand years of intense rivalry between the two nations is behind this phenomenon), the
Frenchman is always the most pompous looking.

In the seventeenth century France, incarnated in
and symbolized by Versailles and Louis XIV, dominated Europe militarily and culturally for the first
time; and it is in this period that France first began its
long and highly successful tradition—a tradition
which is an integral dimension of the importance accorded literature in France to this day and the effect
Sartre had on the French public—of exporting its high
culture abroad as an instrument of its prestige and
power. (The success of this habit even today has enabled the French to continue to impose French at the
United Nations as the second major diplomatic language in a manner that is entirely out of proportion to
France's real power in the world. This is equally true
of the extraordinarily inflated enrollment figures for
French in undergraduate foreign language programs
in American universities at a time when Russian, Ara-
bic, Chinese, and Japanese, could all plausibly claim
vastly greater practical relevance and, at the very
least, equal cultural interest.) In the eighteenth century the awareness of the importance of literature as
an integral part of the political battlefield continued
undiminished. Voltaire would divide his time between
being adored and pampered by the royal courts of
France, England, and Prussia, and cooling his heels in
the royal prison, the Bastille (twice), or going into several exiles; and Diderot would get away with pinching
the thighs of Catherine the Great of Russia in the heat
of philosophical discussion. Indeed, most importantly
of all (a fact which French rulers have never forgot-

ten), writers like these would be credited with contributing to the climate of thought and opinion which eventually helped make the French Revolution of 1789 possible.

C. France's Difficult Accession to Modern Bourgeois Civil Society

This background of state involvement in cultural production really only sets up a context in which some important factors assume greater importance than they would otherwise have had. Just as the unification of France into a successfully centralized absolutist state was more protracted, more violent, and with more detours along the way than similar processes in other great European absolutist powers like England and Spain (but less so than in Russia, which France, and the situation of the French writer, most closely resemble in remarkable fashion), so the revolutionary transformation of the absolute monarchy into a modern capitalist society culturally and politically dominated by an urban bourgeoisie was more traumatic and drawn-out than elsewhere in Europe. England effected the shift in some fifty years between the outbreak of the Civil War and the Glorious Revolution of 1688, and the country was only really at war with itself for a few years during all this period. Italy and Germany compressed their unification into a few violent years in the third quarter of the nineteenth century. (The subsequent fascist interludes in these two countries were desperate solutions to economic crises provoked by working-class militancy in the face of a bourgeois-capitalist order already solidly in place.) For all kinds of reasons—among which was the fact that in France social class battle lines were more sharply drawn—the process in France was more bloody. The great revolution of 1789 lasted longer and was much more radical, as it spun leftward under the impact of foreign invasion, in its challenge to existing social institutions than anything Europe had seen or would see until the Paris Commune of 1871 and the Russian Revolution of 1917. The revolution itself was only brought to a close by the establishment of Napoleon's military dictatorship. The nearly twenty years of constant warfare which followed—in the course of which French revolutionary thought was carried to all corners of Europe—confirmed the French in their belief that they were the schoolmasters of Europe (a belief they are far from having lost). Fresh revolutionary outbreaks would take place in 1830, 1848, and 1871 (the last two being extremely bloody); and even the relative institutional stability of the last hundred years (excluding the hiatus of the German occupation during World War II) does not compare with the extraordinary stability of the state in Britain and the United States. Once again, in 1968, France came close to revolution, surpassing all its European neighbors in the violence with which it registered the social distress from which it was suffering as a result of the transition (which the West as a whole was going through) from a highly conformist mass society, built primarily upon mass-industrial production, to a permissive services–information based economy of endless consumerism.

So eventful and tormented a national history in which "the political" constantly impinged upon daily life in a way much more massively evident than in the

United States, for example—where it is possible to live with the delusion that private and public existence are two distinct domains—has left its mark on French culture in obvious ways. Whereas in the United States— as Sartre, like other French commentators on American society, would point out—it is considered in many circles to be in bad taste to raise political issues at social gatherings (partly because of the sharpness with which ethnic and racial battle lines are drawn in the country); and whereas in the United States it is also considered a sign of weakness and failure to grumble or complain about anything at all (both because of the cult of individualism, according to which the responsibility for misfortune is laid at the door of the person in question, and because criticism and pessimism are bad for the investment climate and consumer spending); and whereas in general the kind of breezy heartiness exemplified by Ronald Reagan characterizes the tone of American life to the foreigner; so constant acrimonious polemic and dissension typify the French. Political campaigns make the recent "negative" American presidential campaign look tame by comparison, and the general tone of political discussion in all walks of life is mostly one of outraged indignation at the turpitude and criminal folly of one's opponents. (This is only now just starting to change: witness the recent experiment in "cohabitation" between the socialist president, François Mitterand, and the conservative premier, Jacques Chirac.) Friendships are made and terminated over political issues: thus Sartre would either break with or be dumped in his turn by people like Camus, Koestler, Aron, and many others, and the meetings of the great surrealist discussion groups would frequently end in brawls over intellectual differences.

For all these reasons, and others too complex to go into here, French writers have been more inclined than those of other nationalities to assume the role already demanded by literary modernism in all the Western countries: the writer as a provocative *enfant terrible,* representative of a subversive and scandalous avant-garde. Important sectors of the French thinking public *expect* their writers to be eccentric nuisances. French literature, especially since the middle of the nineteenth century, is littered with figures playing this role, from Baudelaire to Rimbaud, from surrealism to Sartre. (It is no chance occurrence that the two most scandalous figures of European literature—the Marquis de Sade and Genet—were both Frenchmen.) And politics has always been at the center of French literature in an overt way and to an extent that it has not been in most other Western literary traditions. Many French literary figures have taken intensely unpopular public stands on political issues (Voltaire, Zola, Gide, Sartre, Simone de Beauvoir, Genet), and some have been executed for their positions (for example, Brasillach, who collaborated with the Nazis in the Second World War). But it is not even a matter of French writers being unusually predisposed to engaging in political affairs "outside" of literature: the great nineteenth-century French novelists, Stendhal and Balzac, produced works which were intensely and self-consciously political statements on the historical changes taking place in France at the time, quite unlike anything to be found, for example, in the established canon of American or British literature of the same period. And even when politics was not the overt concern of a writer, its exclusion from literature as an explicit topic often had to be justified by some grand theoretical statement which enabled it to be banished rather than simply ignored as in other countries (Mallarmé, for example). Alternatively a writer like Flaubert, who detested and despised politics, nonetheless felt its pressure as an aesthetic imperative in the French tradition sufficiently to find it necessary, in *The Sentimental Education,* to discredit and disqualify politics as one more human delusion. In our own time the most important and influential aesthetic movement of the twentieth century, surrealism, would be marked by a tormented and endlessly debated relation to revolutionary Marxism.

It should be emphasized that none of this historical context made Sartre a necessary, or inevitable, outcome. Not all French writers, and not even all Sartre's immediate contemporaries, have been politically engaged in the way Sartre was; but it certainly made his career a possibility which a young writer, with the requisite personal history and ambition, could forge. (The emphasis placed, in this series of introductions to writers, on the broad cultural and historical backgrounds of the writers in question, means that we cannot investigate the personal existential adventure whereby Sartre turned himself into a great writer with all the characteristics peculiar to him alone.)

D. "History Flowed in Upon Us ..."

As if it were not enough that Sartre be a product of the tradition described above, his mature works were written over a period dominated by the great conflicts of the Second World War and the Cold War—a period when, as a writer in France, one was under intense pressure to take sides on behalf of fascism or communism, capitalism or communism, and so on. Sartre himself would describe this context most eloquently:

From 1930 on, the world depression, the coming of Nazism, and the events in China opened our eyes. It seemed as if the ground were going to fall from under us, and suddenly, for us too, the great historical juggling began. The first years of the great world Peace [after the end of the First World War] suddenly had to be regarded as the years between wars. Each sign of compromise which we had greeted had to be seen as a threat. Each day we had lived revealed its true face; we had abandoned ourselves to it trustingly and it was leading us to a new war with secret rapidity, with a rigor hidden beneath its nonchalant airs. And our life as an individual which had seemed to depend upon our efforts, our virtues, and our faults, on our good and bad luck, on the good and bad will of a very small number of people, seemed governed down to its minutest details by obscure and collective forces, and its most private circumstances seemed to reflect the state of the whole world. All at once we felt ourselves abruptly situated. The detachment which our predecessors were so fond of practicing had become impossible. There was a collective adventure which was taking form in the future and which would be our adventure.... The secret of our gestures and our most intimate designs lay ahead of us in the catastrophe to which our names would be attached. History flowed in upon us; in everything we touched, in the air we breathed, in the page we read, in the one we wrote; in love itself we discovered, like a taste of history, so to speak, a bitter and ambiguous mixture of the absolute and the transitory.[4]

This immediate context, superimposed upon the already existing tradition of the French writer as an unusually political animal, led the immense majority of the writers of an entire generation—both on the right and on the left of the political spectrum—to endow their works with an intensely and overtly political content.

E. "A Patented Corrupter of Youth," "the Gravedigger of the West"[5]: The Literary Modernist as Harbinger of Social Change

More fundamentally, perhaps, Sartre was at one and the same time the product and agent of a social revolution taking place not only in France but in the world at large. For rather more than a hundred years, down to roughly the 1950s, the industrial capitalism of modern Western societies like the United States, France, and Britain functioned in large measure on the basis of the mass production of commodities. Until very recently it was not technologically possible to produce commodities for a wide variety of taste (or even shape and size, in clothing for example) without incurring considerable additional expense which would have put one out of business. The result was that these societies needed, at a very vital level, to be profoundly conformist, indeed, mass-conformist. The feel of the world these societies created can still be got from films like King Vidor's *The Crowd,* Chaplin's *Modern Times,* footage of Hitler's mass rallies, Sartre's *Nausea,* or simply archival photographs of streets filled with thousands of men all going to work in the same uniform of dark suit, tie, and bowler hat. As is well known, the mass media and entertainment industries sprang up in order to produce this crucially important consensus as to what constituted the desirable in an age when modernity itself had progressively dissolved the traditional values and customs which had formerly ensured social order in the premodern societies which preceded the emergence of nascent capitalism in the Renaissance. A mass medium with these objectives, however, cannot afford on the whole much in the way of excellence. It cannot afford a great deal of inquiring intelligence, for example, or anything that might put in question the dreary round of money-making and modest futile consumption on which such a world is necessarily premised. Mostly it will not go beyond fantasy fulfillments of frustrated desire and the careful production of new desires to fuel the market. Under these circumstances genuine art—that is to say, something which is intelligent, something which puts the world as a whole in question, something which is beautiful and strong and takes your breath away, as opposed to merely distracting you—genuine art in such a world is increasingly ghettoized; it has difficulty finding a public. It is for this reason, in this period, that we first find the popular myth (which has its basis in reality) of the artist (writer, musician, etc.) as a mad genius who dies unappreciated and penniless. Van Gogh is the model here. In these circumstances art becomes oppositional, a more or less explicit contestation and rejection of mainstream "bourgeois society" and a utopian demand for everything denied by the dreary mediocre bourgeois world of work and middle-class family life as functional adaptations to that society. Sartre himself adopted this oppositional stance in an exemplary manner, living out of cheap hotels without a family (but with many lovers) or material possessions (for many years without so much as a personal library), squandering or giving away the considerable fortune he earned as a famous writer, declining the honors society bestowed on him (the Nobel Prize, the *Légion d'Honneur*), adopting political positions far to the left of the French Communist Party, intervening on behalf of political prisoners on both sides of the Iron Curtain, and so on.

In much the same way as Rousseau, Voltaire, and others had helped lay the groundwork for a political revolution in 1789 at the level of political awareness, the utopian demands of much of literary modernism (figures as diverse as Joyce, Gide, Lawrence, Kafka, Sartre, the surrealists) paved the way for the great wave of generalized revolt and upheaval that characterized the 1960s in the industrial West. Which is not at all to suggest that someone like Sartre actually caused the May 1968 insurrection in Paris, or that D. H. Lawrence directly produced the demand for "free love" in the 60s. Simply, with the enormous economic expansion and concomitant rise in standards of living that occurred in the twenty years after the Second World War, and with the relative saturation of the automobile and household-goods markets that had occurred by the 60s and the corresponding urgent need to create new desires and new markets, it became an economic necessity to promote a new kind of individ-

17

ual: someone less subordinate to the conformism of mass-industrial economic production with the quasi-military discipline of the assembly line and morose dedication to sacrifice in the name of more and more production of goods and profit. What the economy needed increasingly was high consumer spending, self-indulgence, much more freedom to pursue avenues of pleasure that had not previously even been marketed. At the same time, the economy expanded to take more and more women into the work force. Contraception, abortion rights, new sexual freedoms, and new conceptions of the family became functional necessities. Which is why the (originally) middle-class nuclear family of a working father, housewife, and children is now a minority phenomenon. In the course of these upheavals the utopian demands of artistic modernism—the legitimation of sexuality which was neither exclusively conjugal nor heterosexual and freedom from the bourgeois nuclear family, freedom in dress codes and body language, a carnivalization of daily life by music and color and a restoration of the rights of the "irrational" psychic dimensions of dream and phantasy, and so on—these demands were taken up and pressed by a generation which radicalized the new forms solicited by the economy and which believed that the political means to implement them were present. The ensuing conflicts provoked by resistance to these changes by an older generation formed by mass conformism constituted the convulsive 60s as entire societies changed gear, without, however, the fundamental transformations of the social order that the utopian demands had implicitly originally entailed. The yuppie 80s—which enjoyed all the freedoms demanded in the

60s, but exclusively at the level of "private space" (and, above all, primarily as commodities)—are as grotesquely diminished a version of what the hippie 60s, at their best, had hoped for as the bourgeois civil society of nineteenth- and twentieth-century France has been a sad caricature of what Rousseau had envisioned in *The Social Contract*.

As we shall see in detail below, both the aggressiveness of Sartre's writing and the violence of the reactions his writing unleashed are to be attributed primarily to the fact that his work—as early as the 1930s—anticipated, projected, and solicited these very social upheavals.

NOTES

1. These two reactions are representative of the violently contradictory responses to Sartre. The first, uttered by President de Gaulle, made in response to pressure to have Sartre arrested, is actually disingenuous. De Gaulle knew perfectly well that such a move would have been politically disastrous—giving Sartre the perfect opportunity to place the French Fifth Republic, rather than himself, on trial—and so attempted by this remark to turn his impotence into a gesture of recognition of Sartre's intellectual merits and cultural importance, something de Gaulle was perfectly incapable of appreciating. In its very opportunism, however, the remark does indicate the very real respect in which Sartre was held, for the remark attempts to get some of this respect to rub off on its author.

The second sentence was chanted by French army veterans marching down the Champs-Elysées, on the occasion of Sartre's denunciations of the French colonial presence in Algeria and his call to young Frenchmen to refuse conscription to serve in the military suppression of the Algerian insurrection.

2. In this section I am indebted to the very useful comparative account of the rise of the modern state in the countries of Europe by

Perry Anderson, *Lineages of the Absolutist State* (London: New Left Books, 1974).

3. Quoted in Léon H. Vincent, *The French Academy* (Boston: Houghton Mifflin, 1901) 70.

4. Jean-Paul Sartre, *Situations II* (Paris: Gallimard, 1948) 242–43.

5. Uttered by the Christian existentialist, Gabriel Marcel, on the occasion of Sartre's declining the Nobel Prize (Gabriel Marcel,"Prise de position," *Nouvelles Littéraires,* 29th Oct. 1964).

CHAPTER TWO

Nausea

Nausea is Sartre's best-known novel: Sartre himself thought of it as his best literary work. It is, with Camus's *l'Etranger,* probably the twentieth-century novel most frequently assigned to students of the period; and it is also more fundamental to an understanding of Sartre's work and the period in which he was writing than anything else he wrote. For all of these reasons there are good grounds for devoting more space and time to *Nausea* than to any other Sartre work.

A. Understanding the Novel on Its Own Terms: Its Axiology or Hierarchical Structure of Oppositions and Resemblances[1]

We shall analyze the work in roughly the order in which it is presented to us.

Nausea is written as a diary or journal kept by one Antoine Roquentin—a bachelor in his thirties of independent if modest means who, after various travels around the world, is writing the biography of an eighteenth-century diplomat and intriguer, the Marquis de Rollebon, in the provincial French town of Mudville, where the Marquis's papers happen to be housed in the municipal library. Roquentin has begun keeping a journal in order to try and clarify to himself, and come to terms with, certain peculiar and faintly alarming changes that have started taking place in his perceptions of the most banal and everyday phenomena:

> I must tell how I see this table, the street, people, my packet of tobacco, since *that* is what has changed. I must determine the exact extent and nature of this change (N 1).

In this opening entry in the diary he cites the first example of the kind of thing that has been happening to him:

> On Saturday the kids were throwing flat stones across the surface of the water, making them ricochet, and I wanted to throw a pebble into the sea like them. Just at that moment I stopped, I dropped the pebble and I left. I must have looked out of it, probably, because the kids laughed behind my back (N 2).

In the next entry, some days later, Roquentin notes that he has now experienced a reassuring return to normal, and that he feels faintly ridiculous about what he had described in the first entry. He describes himself as now being "comfortably and solidly anchored in a respectable everyday bourgeois world" (N 2). He concludes by declaring himself cured, and he renounces recording his daily impressions "as young girls do, in a fine new notebook" (N 3). He has spoken too soon, of course, and the strange impressions return.

What is important at this stage is that Sartre has deliberately provided us with an important opposition—that between being in the world in a solidly bourgeois sort of way and the strange novel sensation, or mode of existence, that is bothering Roquentin—in terms of which we will be able progessively to arrive at an understanding of the book. (All literary works are best understood at a first, purely formal, level—that is, on their own terms as intentional, carefully controlled systems of aesthetic effects designed to solicit a very specific response from the reader—in terms of structured series of oppositions of differences and resemblances. Some of the other means of understanding a literary work we shall deploy in subsequent sections of this chapter.)

In other words, it is Sartre's intention that our gradual understanding of Roquentin's strange sensation be achieved at least in part through a progessive unfolding of that with which it is constantly implicitly contrasted—"normal" bourgeois existence. This starts to become clear in the fourth entry: Roquentin is seated in the Café Mably, and he reflects that "in cafés everything is always normal." He observes the clientele and reflects that "in order to exist, they have to get together as several people before they can even manage it." The opposite of normal existence is immediately indicated: "I, on the other hand, live entirely alone. I speak to no one, ever; I receive nothing, I give nothing" (N 6). The opposition between normal gregariousness and eccentric solitude is then accentuated by the following passage in which Roquentin tries to evoke the character of his thought processes which he contrasts deliberately with the facile narratives he hears from the surrounding customers:

> I marvel at these young people: drinking their coffee, they tell clear, plausible anecdotes. If you ask them what they did yesterday, they are not at a loss: they

bring you up to date in a few words. In their place, I'd have difficulty knowing what to say. It's true that, for a long time now, no one has bothered himself anymore with how I fill my days. When one lives alone, one no longer knows what it is to recount events: the plausible disappears at the same time as friends (N 7).

We now have a great deal to go on. Our series of oppositions has been enriched and complicated to the point where we can already draw up a provisional list to which we can add as we proceed. Under *Strange New Sensation* we can list: 1) an inability to respond to objects and to use them in the ways in which others conventionally do so (e.g. the pebble); 2) existence no longer seems "normal"; 3) solitude; 4) thought processes are ephemeral, elusive, shapeless, and vague; 5) the conventional notion as to what is realistic, plausible, or credible, has become doubtful, and under these circumstances narrative itself becomes problematic. Under *Normal Bourgeois Existence,* by contrast, we can list: 1) objects do not present a problem—one uses them in the way one is supposed to, as they normally present themselves to us, without asking any unnecessary questions about them; 2) existence seems normal; 3) existence seems normal above all because one is with other people; 4) existence is normal when one is with other people because the conventional values shared by a group enable the members to bounce the credible, plausible, socially acceptable versions of the meaning of existence back and forth among the members of the group: on this basis narrative becomes possible (because narrative, to be comprehensible to its audience, must share with them a set of conventions—

common notions as to the identity of entities in the world, the identity and meaning of the world itself, how stories are narrated, and so on).

In contrast to the reassuring conformist blather of the café, in which each participant is able "to recognize joyfully that they are of the same opinion" (N 8), Roquentin contrasts the lonely derelict retired schoolmaster he recalls from his childhood who terrified children, as he sat sunning himself in the Luxembourg Gardens, because they suspected that he "formed the kinds of thoughts that crabs or lobsters have" (N 9; Alexander's English translation reads "thoughts *of* crab," which is incorrect). That which is contrasted with normal bourgeois existence has acquired a fresh component: bestiality or subhumanity of an especially ancient and primitive variety.

A couple of pages later the connection between the strange new sensation in Roquentin's life and *nausea* (which is what we can call the experience from henceforth) is made for the first time:

> Now I see; I remember better what I felt the other day at the edge of the sea when I held that pebble in my hand. It was a kind of sickly-sweet disgust. How unpleasant it was! And it came from the pebble, I'm sure of it, it passed from the pebble into my hands. Yes, that's it, that's just it: a kind of nausea in the hands (N 10–11).

Clearly something rather more than what we ordinarily understand by this term is intended, although what the term really means only becomes clear gradually in the course of the novel. Nausea begins to invade more and more domains of Roquentin's existence: thus, the skepticism which he had brought to bear, under its influence, on the innocent conversations and tales of the clientele of the Café Mably assails in its turn his own project—the biography of the Marquis de Rollebon:

> Well, yes: he could have done all that, but it has not been proved: I'm beginning to believe that one can never prove anything. These are honest hypotheses which take the facts into account: but I feel so sharply that they come from me, that they are quite simply a way of unifying what I know. Not a glimmer comes from Rollebon himself. Slow, lazy, sullen, the facts adapt themselves to the rigor of the order which I want to give them; but it remains external to them. I have the feeling of producing a work of pure imagination (N 13).

Increasingly bored by, and doubtful of, the project, he gets to his feet and examines himself in the mirror in his room. He describes his face as appearing to himself as a faintly obscene, quivering, inhuman, lunar landscape which he has difficulty in recognizing as his own, and which is so boring that he almost falls asleep while examining it.

Far from describing an extraordinary experience at the outer limits of human experience, Sartre is in fact merely trying to dramatize a kind of activity in which we have all engaged at some time or another, especially during our childhood. To take the above example of Roquentin's examination of his reflection in the mirror: most people see their faces in the course of checking on their appearances—with a greater or lesser degree of narcissistic self-involvement, depending on the individual—with a view to maintaining these appearances in the face of others. In other words, the various details of our faces are not usually contemplated in and for themselves as mere things that just happen to be lumped together in a purely contingent and meaningless combination of blotches of color or hunks of bone and meat. On the contrary, generally speaking, our contemplation of our faces is organized by an aesthetic project—"Hmmm ... time I got my hair cut again," or, "Hell, am I really that old?" or, "Is that new lipstick really me?" This more-or-less anxious self-examination is simultaneously a function of what we have internalized from those around us (our looks have been judged attractive or otherwise on the basis of whatever transient standards of physical beauty happen to be prevailing where and when we live) and our attempts—a function of what we have internalized—to capitalize on, or desperately redeem, what we have been endowed with. The specific details of our faces are examined and organized perceptually around these attempts: "Perhaps my chin won't appear to jut out so much if I wear my hair up," for example. In short, our contemplation of our faces is generally a function of a *project*—a fact which is best exemplified by the fact that more contemplations of the mirror take place immediately before we leave our homes *before going to do something else* than at any other time.

All Sartre ever does in order to evoke nausea or the *absurd,* as it is later also called in the book, with regard to something, is *suspend the project which is implicit in the contemplation of the object in question.* Once we have understood this, we hold the key to the whole book. To return to the example of Roquentin's contemplation of his image in the mirror: it is clear that the kind of scrutiny to which he subjects his face cannot serve any cosmetic purpose. The gaze which examines the various features of the face does not, for example, attempt to organize them in a whole—an organization which is essential to an aesthetic assessment (any nose which may be "handsome" on one face can always conceivably be rendered "ugly" by adding it to just the "wrong" combination of surrounding features). Furthermore, Roquentin brings his face far too close to the mirror for an aesthetic contemplation—unless, that is, it had been his intention to squeeze a pimple, in which case such proximity would be the *consequence* of an aesthetic assessment operated at the correct distance (that of a third party) along the lines of "Time to squeeze that pimple." Clearly, this contemplation takes place as an outcome of *boredom,* for want of anything better to do. It is a form of the most archaic and primitive form of *play* engaged in by all human beings, but more especially by children: a haphazard exploration or manipulation of whatever elements may be at hand—above all, in a manner which runs counter to conventional modes of usage (this is why babies or untrained animals "create havoc")—in order to uncover some form of diversion or pleasure; a variety of play which has not, however, been organized into a *game,* entailing partners (poker) or perhaps merely socially codified rules (solitaire). To this extent there remains a project underlying the activity (that of seeking amusement or diversion). The project is minimal, however: one might even say that this kind of behavior represents a *search for a project*—the project immediately preceding this kind of play having dissolved as a

consequence of boredom (or completion or failure)—a
kind of random scanning behavior, picking over the
environment and its possibilities in search of some new
stimulus to organized meaningful activity with which
to occupy the individual. The perfect example of this
kind of activity is what one did as a child when one
took a word like *bread* and repeated it over and over
to oneself until the meaning of the word as a conventional signifier dissolved into a meaningless lumpy
doughy consistency in one's mouth which no longer
bore any resemblance to one's normal use of the word,
even though one was continuing to pronounce the word
correctly (albeit with increasing difficulty). The point
at which one had reduced the word to real meaninglessness was always distinctly pleasurable because the
word had come to acquire a kind of virgin strangeness
and novelty that was diverting—a tiny adventure in
the midst of the oceanic infantile boredom in which one
so often found oneself. The progressive estrangement
of the word in these conditions is the simple result of
its systematic misuse: normally when we use the word
we neither see nor hear it—which is not to say that it
is normally invisible or inaudible: simply, when we
say, for example, "Joe, pass the bread, please," or, "I
hate bread," we do not concern ourselves with the material auditory dimensions of the word beyond making
sure that we have enunciated them correctly. The letters, *b, r, e, a, d,* in other words, in and of themselves
as material entities, have nothing to do with the real
material object bread itself: the word *bread* is simply
a conventional instrument we make use of in order to
achieve practical and expressive ends. The ultimate
proof that the word itself has nothing to do with the

material object is to be found in the fact that the same signifying operation can be performed in any one of the world's hundreds of different languages. This is what we mean when we say that normally we do not see, hear, or feel the word *bread* when we speak it but instead transcend the material dimension of the word toward its signification; unless, for example, we are non-native speakers of English and have to make a special effort to pronounce the word correctly in order to avoid embarrassing misunderstandings. On the other hand, when, as bored children, we say "bread, bread, bread" ad infinitum, we are deliberately doing the exact opposite of the normal conventional operation: by "mindlessly" repeating the word in the absence of anything remotely to do with bread, by relentlessly foregrounding its material dimension, we effectively evacuate all meaning from it because no context could conceivably endow such behavior with signifying significance; (on the contrary, the traditional stereotypical representation of madness is the lunatic huddled in the corner muttering the same word over and over). Our parents soon taught us that this kind of behavior is "absurd," or "silly." And so indeed it may well be. When mobilized as a systematic and controlled literary experiment, however, this behavior affords some powerful and interesting effects.

This is essentially the move Sartre makes every time he wishes to evoke what at this stage he calls "nausea" and which he will later describe as the "absurd"—whether it is a question, as here, of Roquentin's face, a bartender's suspenders, or, most notoriously, in the most celebrated scene in the novel, a chestnut tree in a public park. An especially good example of this procedure is to be found a few pages after Roquentin's encounter with his image in the mirror. He is seated in the Café Rendezvous des Cheminots. To the right of him a small group of men is playing a game of cards:

The cards fall on the woollen cloth, spinning. Then the hands with ringed fingers come and pick them up, scratching the cloth with their nails. The hands make white splotches on the cloth, they look puffy and dusty. Other cards continue to fall, the hands come and go. What a strange occupation: it doesn't look like a game, or a rite, or a habit. I think they do this quite simply in order to fill time. But time is too wide, it doesn't allow itself to be filled. Everything which one plunges into it goes limp and stretches out. That gesture, for example, of the red hand, which picks up the cards while fumbling: it is all flabby. It would have to be unstitched and tailored inside (N 20–21).

A couple of pages later he describes the card game a second time:

"*Voilà!*"

A voice rises from the tumult. It is my neighbor who is speaking, the scarlet-faced old man. His cheeks make a violet stain on the brown leather of the bench. He slaps a card down on the table. The ten of diamonds.

But the young man with a head like a dog's smiles. The flushed player, bent over the table, watches him, ready to pounce.

"*Et voilà!*"

The hand of the young man rises from the shadow,

glides an instant, white, indolent, then plunges suddenly like a hawk and presses a card against the cloth. The fat red-faced man jumps up:
"Shit! He's trumped" (N 22–23).

What is striking, and important, about these descriptions is the contrast that Sartre deliberately sets up between two passages which describe exactly the same activity in completely different terms. In the first passage the activity of the participants in the card game is studiously presented in terms that make it appear inhuman: the hands are evoked in such a way as to seem detached from human bodies or human intention; they could almost be small animals or crabs scurrying about on the table, engaged in activity which is enigmatic to the observer. In short, the goals of this behavior, the *project* which underlies it—winning at a game of cards—has been carefully excised from the passage. This is what endows the activity in question with its faintly absurd, purely mechanical, or dreamlike quality. In the second passage, on the other hand, we see the faces of the participants, we hear their excited voices (faces and voices are traditional indices of meaning and intention), the hands are carefully attached to their owners ("the hand of the young man" etc.), and we learn the identities of the cards as they are played as meaningful, intentional bids and ripostes in the course of organized competitive activity ("Shit! He's trumped!").

Why this marked difference between the two passages? And why describe the same scene over twice?

The first passage is preceded by Roquentin's arrival at the Rendezvous des Cheminots, to which he has come in order to sleep with its proprietor, Françoise, as is his wont. She is out, however. The sharp sexual disappointment he experiences plunges him into a fresh attack of "nausea" because it entails the removal of the immediate, short-range meaning of his life, which is sleeping with Françoise. We have all experienced the initial moment of floundering around which one experiences when frustration of one's intention leaves one, temporarily, with a sense of "What the hell am I supposed to do next?" One's energies have been so narrowly concentrated upon one specific goal that the sudden impossibility of realizing it temporarily drains all meaning from life, while one reluctantly tries to regroup one's energies and focus them upon some new objective. This is all the more true for Roquentin to the extent that he is an atheist—in other words, his life has no sanction and no meaning other than those he chooses or those the culture in which he lives endows it with; and such meaning as he does have in his life—the biography of the Marquis de Rollebon— is increasingly tenuous and suspect in his own eyes. For all of these reasons everything in the café, including the card game, is, in Roquentin's eyes, blighted by meaninglessness—that is, is not justified by being organized around a project of his.

So, why does the second description of the card game differ so markedly from the first? What has happened in the interim, what has caused Roquentin's perception of the identical phenomenon to change so fundamentally, is that he has asked the waitress to play his favorite record, the jazz song "Some of These Days." The ensuing description of the music and the effect it has on Roquentin—and the assumptions about existence and art in general which underpin this description—are crucially important for an understanding of the novel. First of all, the notes of the music are described as being integrated into "an inflexible order" which prevents them from ever "existing for themselves" (N 21). In other words, the individual notes of the music cannot be apprehended independently of the melody in which they participate: if one were to change any one of the notes of the melody, one would have a mistake, a discordance, at worst, or a different melody at best. Furthermore, each note has to be sacrificed to the ensuing ones (dwelling longer than the score requires on any one note would destroy or change the melody just as changing one of the notes would). In short, each note—while it could, in principle, be played separately (in a music theory class, for example)—here and now, in the *Rendezvous des Cheminots,*—must and can only be heard as *existing-for-the- sake-of-the-melody*. Music, in other words, presents the listener with the possibility of redeeming the fallen world of existence which "*exists for itself.*" We have seen how things—pebbles, faces, words, and so on—when the human projects which endow them with meaning are suspended, can acquire a depressing pointlessness, an absurdity, a merely contingent status; the aesthetic experience, the rapt attention to music, however, affords a magical utopian respite from the constant threat of nauseating absurdity because, in order to be apprehended for what it is—that is to say, *music,* a carefully ordered series of notes to be perceived as a meaningful totality (a melody) rather than a haphazard jumble of sounds—a musical composition has to be perceived as meaningful *in order to be heard*. If not, one does not hear the music; one simply hears a cacophony.

The "necessity of this music" (the necessary role which each note, its relative volume, its duration, play in the total effect which emerges as "Some of These Days"), changes Roquentin's relations to his environment: the passage of time, for example, is evoked in completely different ways in the two descriptions of the card game. In the first, time is described as too vast to be able to be filled by a mere card game; everything which enters temporality under the dominion of the absurd, of nausea, which is the "slimy pool" of human time, "our time," becomes "soft ... spreads" (N 21), becomes "flabby." In the second description, in which the music plays simultaneously with the card game, the rigorous order of the music—which is counterposed to the flabbiness of ordinary lived time (it is described as a "band of steel," "this hardness")—transforms Roquentin's way of being-in-the-world:

What has just happened is that the Nausea has disappeared. When the voice rose, in the silence, I felt my body harden and the Nausea vanished. Suddenly it was almost painful to become all hard like that, all brilliant burning red. At the same time the music was drawn out, it swelled like a waterspout.... My beer glass has shrunk, it huddles on the table: it seems dense, indispensable. I want to pick it up and feel the weight of it, I stretch out my hand ... My God! *That's* what has changed more than anything else, it's my gestures. This movement of my arm has developed like a majestic theme.... Adolphe's face is there.... At the instant that my hand was closing,

I saw his head; it had the obviousness, the necessity of a conclusion (N 22).

In Sartrean terms art (music, painting, literature etc.), as exemplified here, dispels nausea because the latter is the experience, in a godless world (this is obviously a crucial proviso), of the ultimate unjustifiability of all being: the fact that things simply *are* for no apparent reason, that they exist in a manner that is merely contingent, devoid of the necessity which divine creation (or the rigor of mathematical logic) bestows. For as long as we are caught up in our ephemeral and trivial projects, we manage to impose a transient meaning and order upon the great undifferentiated mass of being: my face's stupid lumpish *isness* does not manifest itself to me as long as I merely look at it as an element in the world I am trying to deal with—a face to serve or betray me in the pursuit of the realization of my desires. As soon, however, as these projects dissolve (in an access of profound despair or boredom, for example), then the baffling enigma of existence (Why is there something rather than nothing?) assails one. Art's utopian redemptive function, according to Sartre's aesthetic, resides in its presenting us with an imaginary microcosm, a fleeting recreation of the world in which *all* its elements are suffused with necessity by virtue of each dimension of the work's indispensability to all the others. Whereas in a godless world it is perfectly possible to imagine the universe continuing to exist and function without me, or even without the planet Earth and its life forms, the jazz song "Some of These Days" (or the novel *Nausea,* for that matter) would no longer be what it is if any of its integral parts, even one note, were changed. Each note of the song is necessary, sanctioned, legitimized, by the whole of which it is a part; just as, in the cosmos of medieval Christianity, every aspect of the creation had its role to play in the divine order of things. (In this respect *Nausea* can be said to constitute a perfect example of modern humanity's will to replace God by humankind as the measure of the world; it is also an example of the way in which, in the modern age, art comes to replace religion as the most precious repository of the society's central interrogations and understanding of being; but more of this later [see section C of this chapter]).

To listen to music or read a novel, and be alive to its aesthetic beauty, then, is, according to Sartré, to *totalize* a multiplicity of details, to perceive all the details of the work in question as forming a meaningful whole. To fail to do this is to be incapable of perceiving the work's beauty: as we have seen, one would not be able even to hear music, for example, instead of mere noise. Furthermore, this totalization is always also a totalization *of the world:* for the duration of one's immersion in a novel, for example (especially if one's reading takes place without critical distance, or if this critical distance is only intermittent), one has to subscribe to the version of the world which the novelist presents to us for our credulity and endorsement. Even if we find ourselves loathing everything the novelist stands for (his or her implicit political values as they express themselves in the representation of character, for example), in an initial moment we have to be the novelist's accomplice in the bringing into being of the imaginary world that is presented to us by the text. Only once we have done this can we then mutter to ourselves, "Racist cretin!" and so on.

One proof that art always entails a totalization of the world is that political or religious controversy—even censorship by the powers that be—has frequently followed upon the production of great works of art. That music entails a totalization of the world is less obviously true but no less so. The totalization implied by music is essentially the mood it solicits: thus, to take a familiar example, the music of Beethoven implies that human destiny, albeit deeply tragic, nonetheless remains titanically heroic and ultimately noble; furthermore, the boundless audacity of this music, its astonishing innovations and transformation of the Western musical tradition on which Beethoven was drawing, its grand dramatic gestures—all of this implies a conception of human possibility and the world which is as much political as it is musical. The values implicit in Beethoven's music are very much those of the heroic, triumphant moment of the European bourgeoisie at the turn of the eighteenth and nineteenth centuries. We find very much the same flavor or mood in the contemporary work of Hegel, the epic turmoil and grand drama of the French Revolution, and the career of Napoleon.

It is this totalization of the world—the organization of all its parts into a meaningful whole—effected by music which operates the transformation of the card game from something inhuman and incomprehensible into an intelligible game played by human beings. For the same reason Roquentin is able to view his entire past in a different light. In the very next paragraph after the second description of the card game (the music is still playing), he continues thus:

> I am moved, I feel my body to be like a precision machine at rest. I have had real adventures. I can recapture no detail, but I perceive the rigorous succession of the circumstances. I have crossed the oceans, I have left towns behind me.... I have had women, I have fought with men; and I was never able to go back on any of it, no more able to do so than a record can turn backwards. And *where* was all this leading me? To this very minute, to this bench, to this bubble of light filled with the humming of music (N 23).

This is in significant contrast to Roquentin's irritable reflections after his conversation with the Self-Taught Man in the course of which the latter asks him whether he has had any adventures. He concludes that contrary to his earlier affirmations, he has had none because adventure is a *literary* category rather than an existential one. When one lives, there are no beginnings or endings, no climaxes, no carefully wrought plots because life extends behind us into the past, full of vague periods one can scarcely recall and apparently pointless detours, and open-endedly into the future. To transform lived events into adventures, however, one has merely to narrate them: the essential change resides in surreptitiously including the end of the adventure right at the beginning of the narrative. While one is ostensibly starting at the beginning—"One evening I was walking down Fifth Avenue, bored with life, when ... "—it is in fact the conclusion of the tale which implacably draws the narrative along, organizing its structure and every detail. The reader knows this: for us, the innocuous details of the opening of the tale are already charged with meaning, they are already part of an adventure. For the character who is living the events, however, this is not the case.

The opposition between art and existence is central to *Nausea,* and we shall return to it in due course. Suffice it to say at this stage that it seems clear from what we have seen up to now that Sartre is ambivalent toward art: on the one hand, it represents a redemptive ideal, and one is joyful in its contemplation; on the other, it represents a possible temptation to take refuge in a conception of existence which is illusory—a conception which would fail adequately to distinguish between art and existence, a conception which would seek an erroneous and dishonest consolation for the shapelessness and meaninglessness of existence by assimilating existence to art.

We have here the first mobilization of an organizational opposition which is fundamental to *Nausea* and all the writings of Sartre's early period: the opposition between what he would call elsewhere—in his first great philosophical treatise, *Being and Nothingness*—*bad faith* and *authenticity*. Broadly speaking, bad faith consists in an evasion of an unpleasant truth. As it occurs in this novel, it consists in a refusal to accept, on the one hand, the ultimate meaninglessness of what, in *Being and Nothingness,* is called *being-in-itself* (rocks, trees, tables) and the totality of being as a whole (the universe) and, on the other hand, an unwillingness to accept the fact that such meaning as we do find in the world is solely human in origin or the product of *being-for-itself* (consciousness). The creation of meaning is a manifestation of our freedom, and thereby our responsibility. Thus, to perceive the world, or one's life, as an organized totality on the model of a work of art or the Christian God's creation is, according to Sartre, to avoid confronting the emptiness of the universe and to avoid assuming our authentic freedom and responsibility for such meanings and values as we have formulated. Sartre shares with other existentialists a deep suspicion of conventional social forms of thought and behavior, which he sees as constantly conspiring to evade these threatening truths.

A good example of the kinds of ways in which this opposition between authenticity and bad faith is put to work in the novel occurs immediately after the scene in the Rendezvous des Cheminots we have just examined. Finally exasperated by the people around him, Roquentin walks out into the night and is instinctively drawn to the Boulevard Noir (*noir* means "black" in French), which he describes with satisfaction as a sort of no-man's land, unlit, deserted and disreputable, cold, dark, silent, mineral, inhuman, containing nothing but hard stones. The boulevard is favorably contrasted with the principal commercial streets of the town, which are described as lighted, filled with reassuring domesticated sounds like those of human voices and automobiles, warm, and inhabited by living things, "dogs, men, all the flabby masses which move spontaneously" (N 24). (Clearly, many of the oppositions which we have already identified are being exploited again here.) The boulevard Noir is a relief to Roquentin:

I am won over by the purity of that which surrounds me; nothing is alive; the wind blows, straight lines flee into the night. The boulevard Noir does not have the indecent look of bourgeois streets which display their charms to passersby.... The Nausea has stayed back there, in the yellow light. I am happy: this cold is so pure, this night is so pure; am I not myself a wave of freezing cold air? What it would be to have neither blood, lymph, nor flesh, ... to be simply coldness (N 25–26).

This expression of a desire to be immaterial, above all to transcend *flesh,* is important both as an evocation of Sartre's conception of consciousness and as an indication of Sartre's attitude toward sexuality. We will return to these matters presently. In the meantime, it is just at this point that Roquentin perceives that he is not alone on the boulevard, and he finally recognizes Lucie, the cleaning woman from the cheap hotel where he lives, and her husband. Earlier he had described Lucie briefly, at work cleaning the stairs, complaining to the hotel manageress about her marriage. Roquentin describes her in this earlier scene as suffering "like a miser" (N 11): that is to say, she consistently refuses to acknowledge to herself the degree of her unhappiness and tries to fool herself on this score by discussing her marital problems in a tone of extreme reasonableness, as if she were in fact giving advice to someone else suffering from the problem in question. Here, however, after a brief altercation with her husband, Lucie gives full vent to her suffering, rending the night with her screams. It is clear from the text that Roquentin/Sartre considers Lucie to have attained a degree of authenticity which is not the norm for her. What is important for our purposes is the explanation of this transformation which is furnished: she is described as suffering with "an insane generosity" (N 27), a novel capability that is explained as arising from her being on the Boulevard Noir. The same oppositions we have seen at work up to this point in the novel are invoked here: Lucie is able to accede to this rare and uncharacteristic moment of authenticity because she is removed from a reassuring conventional social environment. The emphasis on the purifying, redemptive inhumanity and minerality of the boulevard and, especially, its hardness (as counterposed to the "flabbiness" of what has been left behind in the town) is intended to make us recall the inhumanity of Roquentin's face as it appeared to him in the mirror (which now appears to us, in the light of this later passage, as incipiently positive rather than merely peculiar). Similarly we recall that the jazz song heard in the café just before this scene was also represented as being hard, a "band of steel," possessed of a temporal dimension which put to shame the flabbiness characteristic of human temporality. Furthermore, this moment in the cold of the Boulevard Noir shares with the audition of the jazz song the distinction of being the only moments in the book up to this point when Roquentin describes himself as being "happy."

At this early stage of the book we are already in possession of the fundamental pattern of oppositions which constitutes the *axiology,* or hierarchy of values, in terms of which the novel has been written and in terms of which it is to be understood at a first elementary level. "Normal" (socially conventional or acceptable) behavior—be it innocent games like skimming

43

flat pebbles across the surface of the sea, or playing cards, or merely taking a drink in a bar—is endowed with a kind of absurdity, a vaguely obscene contingency (it constantly gives rise to the metaphor of an oppressive superabundance of undesirable flesh) which provokes a powerful visceral reaction of disgust, that is to say, nausea. Counterposed to all of this, as a pole of positive contrast, are: 1) art—music and literature (although the latter can present, in certain circumstances, a temptation to inauthenticity, namely, the desire to confuse life and literature)—which possesses the necessary "rigor" (N 37; Alexander's translation misleadingly gives "precision") to redeem the nauseating absurdity of existence by endowing it with aesthetic form and meaning; 2) activities which, from the conventional point of view, are pointless and ill-advised: for example, nocturnal strolls in sinister and physically uncomfortable zones that are marginal to those humanized environments which are our modern cities.

Much of this is reiterated in a long entry of the diary under the heading "Sunday." Roquentin decides to treat himself to the spectacle of the members of the upper classes of Mudville exchanging polite inanities in the Rue Tournebride after Sunday morning mass. The description of the spectacle is preceded by a sarcastic historical and sociological explanation of the presence of the large, and obscenely expensive, church on this particular street—an explanation which enables Roquentin/Sartre to suggest that the church serves not so much as a means of sincere religious belief (Roquentin/Sartre has little time for the latter anyway) as an instrument of political and economic power. He observes the mechanical ritualized gestures of hats being raised, hands being shaken, etc., which, because of the flagrant absence of any real communication taking place (beyond mutual confirmation in a shared sense of superiority) is patently absurd. When his sardonic curiosity has been satisfied, he repairs to the Brasserie Vézelise for lunch. Seated at his table, Roquentin divides his attention between a novel by Balzac, *Eugénie Grandet*—from which a couple of passages are transposed directly into *Nausea* and which evoke the burgeoning love of the innocent and naïve heroine for a young man—and the conversation and behavior of a married couple seated at the next table with which the Balzac passages have been deliberately juxtaposed. It becomes progressively clear that the conversation at the next table involves a malicious and vicarious (preeminently sexual) enjoyment by both parties of the knowledge the husband recounts to his wife of infidelity on the part of mutual acquaintances. At no point does it occur to the couple that their enjoyment of someone else's infidelity casts a shadow on their own marriage because of the implicit acknowledgment that their own marriage cannot be fulfilling if the need for this sordid and malevolent titillation exists. This little scene is one of Sartre's many angry indictments of the institution of bourgeois marriage—an institution which, because of the interpolation of Balzac, it is suggested, is a nineteenth-century fable the reality of which is even more sordid than Balzac himself (scarcely a starry-eyed idealist in these matters) took it to be.

After his meal in the brasserie Roquentin goes for a walk on the jetty of the port, a favorite Sunday afternoon promenade of the townsfolk of all social classes. The choice of locale is significant: on this narrow strip of stone jutting out into the sea, exposed to the open air, bereft of the protective shelter of streets and urban dwellings, the crowd of people is presented to us in a manner that is significantly different from its counterpart of the Rue Tournebride with which we are intended to compare it. In the first place the social composition of the crowd is more mixed: the strict social hierarchy of the Rue Tournebride has disintegrated as the elite rub elbows with lowly employees. Furthermore the individual members of the crowd are now "only men who are almost alone, who are not representative" (N 51), and as we know by now, solitude in *Nausea* is a precondition for authenticity. Clearly this scene, in the axiological topography of *Nausea,* represents a sort of halfway house between the authenticity of the asocial black hole of the Boulevard Noir and the grotesque high society ballet of the Rue Tournebride.

There is a curious little episode at the conclusion to this scene that is worth commenting on, as it serves as the motivation for the next section of the novel. In the gathering dusk of the early evening on the jetty promenade, Roquentin sees a young woman, her lipstick seemingly black on the blue of her face in the evening light (a description which reminds us of an early modernist experiment in painting); and then the lighthouse on an island out in the bay lights up:

> A little boy stopped near me and murmured with an air of ecstasy, "Oh, the lighthouse!"
> Then I felt my heart swell with a great feeling of adventure (N 54).

Roquentin plunges into the night convinced that he is on the brink of an adventure "happy like the hero of a novel"(N 54). Of course, nothing really happens to him. What is important is that we understand why Roquentin is suddenly imbued with this feeling of imminent adventure. What has happened is that, against the background of the almost artistically arranged view of the young woman, an aesthetic appreciation of the entire scene is triggered off by the young boy's rapturous exclamation. It will be recalled that for Sartre the aesthetic experience consists primarily in a totalization of the elements in question (episodes in a novel, blotches of color in a painting, notes in a musical composition) such that each element is significantly and indispensably related to all the others in a total effect which emerges as beauty. As he puts it, while trying to explain his sense of adventure:

> I don't know whether everything in the world has been drawn more tightly together or whether it's me who introduces such a powerful unity between the sounds and the forms: I cannot even conceive that any of that which surrounds me could be other than what it is (N 54).

This admirably captures the sense of the *necessity* of art or beauty. Here it is the proximity of the young woman (who already resembles a modernist painting) and the explicit aestheticization of the scene by the boy which solicits an aesthetic response on the part of Roquentin, a response which, as in his audition of "Some of These Days," solicits in its turn what Sartre has called elsewhere an *imaginarization* of the viewer. We recall that when he heard the jazz song Roquentin (contrary to his conviction as expressed elsewhere) is persuaded that he has had adventures in his life; here too Roquentin yields to the temptation (as we have all done in the presence of stirring music or a stupendously beautiful scene) to include himself in the moving tableau before him and grant himself an attractive (that is to say, essential, necessary) role within the totality in question (the world). This *is* the sense of adventure, the sense that one's life forms a significant totality, a destiny, like the plot of a novel in which each event portends and prepares the next:

> Something comes backward onto the scattered moments of this Sunday and welds them together, gives them a meaning and a direction: I have traversed this whole day only in order to arrive here, with my forehead against this window pane, in order to contemplate this finely featured face blossoming against a red curtain (N 55–56).

Of course, the next morning Roquentin is thoroughly disgusted with himself for having allowed himself to give way to his illusory sense of adventure. He relapses into his dreary existence, trying fitfully and unenthusiastically to continue the biography of Rollebon. At which point he receives a summons from a former lover, Anny, to go up to Paris and meet her a few days later. He recalls her obsession with creating "perfect moments" which are clearly feminine versions of his own masculine "adventures," being based on a similar totalizing aestheticization of the world:

> "Listen, you will make an effort, won't you? You were so stupid last time. You see how this moment

could be beautiful? Look at the sky, look at the color of the sun on the carpet. I have got my green dress on for the occasion and I'm wearing no makeup, I'm all pale. Move back, go and sit in the shadow (N 62).

As Roquentin progressively loses interest in his biography of the Marquis de Rollebon, the impending meeting with Anny will come increasingly to be the sole meaning in his life.

Sartre next engages—with the episodes involving Dr. Roget and Monsieur Fasquelle—a favorite theme of all existentialist writers: death. One can only really understand the centrality of this subject in existentialist writing if one considers it conjointly with the aggressive atheism of most of these writers. Existentialism is above all an attempt to come to terms with a historically novel sense of meaninglessness or absurdity in life following upon the sudden realization at some point in recent history—generally, if somewhat simplistically, identified with Nietzsche's clamorous announcement of the death of God in the late nineteenth century—that the modern world is somehow incompatible with religious belief. If the universe and human destiny are merely contingent accidents entirely bereft of that transcendental or divine design which might endow them with absolute necessity, then such meaning as existence has been declared to have is merely human and relative. Because of the historical and cultural relativity of human belief and custom, anything goes. This is the secret premise of modern liberalism which Nietzsche, seeking to unmask its complacent tolerance, called "the advent of nihilism"—that is, the secret belief in nothing at all beyond that which is dictated by the expediency of the moment.

Now, if the death of God changes the very nature of life, it also introduces a cataclysmic change into human attitudes toward death. The promise of an afterlife has been an immemorial consolation to humanity in the face of death. If this consolation is removed, then death, like life itself henceforth, becomes a deeply unsettling enigma which baffles all understanding. In short, like life, death becomes *absurd*.

Death with the promise of an afterlife is bad enough. Death which is definitive, and which comes after a life that has served no apparent purpose, is an intolerable scandal, an outrage. Which is why our age, more than any other in recorded history, has sought by every possible means to deny the very existence of death. So that it is by no means inconceivable for a person today to go through an entire life without ever having set eyes upon a corpse (excluding, of course, the many thousands which are portrayed with numbing frequency on television). This was impossible in bygone times when death formed an integral part of life (public executions, corpses kept in the home until burial etc.). This denial reaches its apotheosis in the practice of embalming corpses widely prevalent in the United States—a practice that is equally incongruous if one is a believing Christian (for whom the soul alone should count) or if one is an atheist. This practice, therefore, can only serve one purpose: a pathetic and infantile denial of the reality of death in its most obvious and immediate manifestation: the putrefaction of the body.

Heidegger, Camus, Malraux, Sartre, all the writers

and philosophers who were at one time or another labeled existentialists, took the position that for life to
be worthwhile, death must not only be accepted but
embraced. Which is not to suggest that these writers
display a morbid or self-indulgent preoccupation with
death. On the contrary, they all assert, implicitly or
explicitly, that one has to engage with death in order
to live life to the full. Most of us would probably acknowledge, on a moment's reflection, that we rarely
confront the certainty of our demise. We are ready, to
be sure, to recognize as an intellectual proposition the
fact that we will doubtless eventually die. Everyone
does, after all. And we acknowledge the reality of
death when we grow alarmed at some strange physical
symptom we have, or when we wonder, with that nagging fear in our bellies, whether we have AIDS or
whether our smoking habit will lead to cancer. Nonetheless, we scarcely ever really confront death because
most of us, for most of our lives, feel we are in a position to consider it as a score that will only have to be
settled at some distant point in the future; and also
because the idea is anxiety-provoking. This habit is
enervating, however. Some of us have narrowly es-
caped death, or at least known or heard of people who
have done so, and either directly experienced or heard
of the renewed sense of life's preciousness, and its intensity, which is often the (mostly short-lived, to be
sure) outcome of such experiences. In other words, it
is the visceral, rather than merely intellectual, awareness of the fragility of life, of the fact that death can
strike at any time, that it always takes one by surprise
(as in our initial sense of shock and refusal to acknowledge the death of someone close to us, even when the

death in question has been anticipated for a long time), which enhances life and ideally should be sustained. It is this outrageous, the shocking, dimension of death that makes Dr. Roget's "experience"—a cumulative rationalization of existence—so laughable, in Sartre's view, in the face of something (be it life *or* death) which is an unfathomable enigma, a blank "wall," as Sartre characterizes it in a short story of that name.

In short, if we could only learn to live, as popular wisdom has it, "every day as if it were our last," where everything is at stake, where our faculties and our priorities are wonderfully concentrated by the finality, the irredeemability, of our last acts, instead of squandering our lives in lazy mediocrity, we would *really live*. (The extraordinary exhilaration which comes with this embracing of death is more powerfully expressed in a couple of Camus's works—in the conclusion to *The Stranger,* for example, which, contrary to many interpretations, is a white-hot hymn to life, and in the short story *The Unfaithful Wife*—than in anything Sartre ever wrote.) This is the kernel of truth that is contained in the mystifying promise made to kamikaze pilots or Iranian teen-agers being sent on suicide missions that they would go to heaven as martyrs: if you can *willingly* accept to die for the group—even if this acceptance is the product of a manipulation of which you are unaware—then your last hours will indeed be consumed in a blaze of exalted intoxication. (In fact, only in this condition is it possible to perform such an amazing act.)

Needless to say, despite all of this Sartre is true to the choice we all make most of the time: having condemned Dr. Roget for hiding behind his "experience" in the face of death, Roquentin himself promptly goes into a blue funk three days later because he thinks the proprietor of the Café Mably, Monsieur Fasquelle, may have died. Of course, what really unnerves him is not so much the loss of Fasquelle as it is the sudden reminder of death itself.

It is very much with the shocking sense of the absurdity of both life and death in mind that Roquentin next visits Mudville's municipal museum, where he views the stuffy official portraits of the town's worthies and notables. What revolts him in these portraits is that they all radiate a self-important identification with their official, conventional social roles—leadership, paternity, and social rank—an identification which has all too clearly served the individual in question with the means for evading precisely the questions which torment Roquentin. These people have never put themselves in question. Far from finding existence absurd, they consider that they have a "right" to exist by virtue of their social rank, their wealth, and so on. Their confident, arrogant poses represent what Roquentin calls "the reign of the human" (N 90)—that is to say, the most complete negation of the inhuman enigma of existence's absurdity.

This critical gaze brought to bear on the denial of absurdity by others necessarily turns back upon the critic himself: Roquentin realizes that the biography of Rollebon is as unjustifiable and illegitimate a reason for existing as the self-important reasons the elite of Mudville took so seriously. He abandons the biography.

The long scene between Roquentin and the Self-Taught Man is self-explanatory and requires little in

the way of comment beyond the fact that the ideas of
the latter are a kind of caricatural quintessence of the
ideology of the modern liberal bourgeoisie as peddled
by a desperately down-trodden, oppressed, petty bourgeois, would-be ideologue. His "humanism," his faith
in humanity, in progress, above all his faith in knowledge, even his timid and naïve socialism—which deliberately ignores the fact that the social classes in
France are at each other's throats—all this betrays the
Self-Taught Man as a caricature of one of the central
ideologies of modernity (a kind of watered-down and
sugary posterity of Rousseau) which is chiefly represented in the West today by centrist and left-of-center
political parties like the Democratic Party in the
United States or the British Labor Party. (The other
principal component of bourgeois ideology—its pessimistic component, which is invoked when it has been
decided that a period of austerity with respect to social
spending and a period of national asset-stripping are
the order of the day—portrays humanity as innately
egotistical and competitive, requiring rule by an iron
fist if individuals are not to tear one another to pieces.
This ideology derives ultimately from the great ide-
ologues of the absolutist monarchy like Hobbes—
whence its pessimism and emphasis on what we today
call "law and order"—and is today represented in the
West by the political Right.) The Self-Taught Man's
love for humanity—or what he likes to think is love
(naïve idealization of people cannot constitute love;
love accepts the other warts and all, one loves people
as much *for* their faults and foibles as for their virtues)—and his assurance that he is "never alone" will

be cruelly disappointed when he is reduced to the worst kind of solitude—that of being an outcast—by the vicious conformism of the society which cannot tolerate his homosexuality.

After fleeing the company of the Self-Taught Man, Roquentin ends up in the municipal park of Mudville. It is here, in what is the best known and most memorable scene of the whole book, that he will experience the fundamental "enlightenment" (N 127; Alexander has "vision," whereas the French is *illumination*) which brings complete understanding of what this troubling sensation, this nausea, really is. This illumination is motivated by the intense disgust, the overwhelming sense of absurdity, Roquentin feels listening to the high-minded drivel of the Self-Taught Man which attempts to articulate a collective social meaning to existence ("humanity"). The nausea which assails him is so intense that, in the course of the ride in the tram which takes him from the restaurant to the park, "things are freed from their names" (N 125); and Roquentin, in a moment reminiscent of surrealist experiment, contemplates a seat in the tram feeling that it could just as well be a dead donkey floating belly up in a river as what it really is. This is the point of departure for the scene in the park:

> So I was in the park just now. The root of the chestnut tree plunged into the earth, just below my bench. I no longer remembered that it was a root. Words had melted away and, with them, the meaning of things, the ways in which we use them, the feeble points of reference which men have traced on their surfaces (N 126–27).

Roquentin has become so alienated from the society around him that he contests it at that level which is most fundamental to its collective existence: the meaning and identity of objects. What he has discovered is something which we all know; but which we studiously pass over most of the time because, like death, the fact is threatening: existence is something that cannot be explained or circumscribed by our rational discourse of causes and effects, mathematical measurement, and scientific explanation, which we assiduously mobilize in order always to find ourselves facing a world that has been reassuringly humanized:

> I was seeking in vain to *count* the chestnut trees, to *situate* them in relation to the Velleda, to compare their height with that of the plane trees: each one of them escaped from the relations in which I was seeking to enclose it, isolated itself, overflowed the boundaries. I could sense the arbitrary nature of these relations (which I stubbornly persisted in maintaining in order to delay the crumbling of the human world of measures, of quantities, of directions) (N 128).

None of this is able to get a grip on, or do justice to, the astonishing, scandalous, fact *that there is something rather than nothing*.

Modern science can perhaps explain *how* the universe is structured and how it came into being (the Big Bang theory, etc.); but science cannot—as it is presently constituted—explain *why* the process began in the first place. Only religion—disqualified in Roquentin's eyes—claims to do this. Roquentin finally hits upon the word which would subsequently have such a success as an intellectual buzz-word in the period following the Second World War: existence is *absurd*. A circle in pure geometry, as Roquentin explains it to us, is not absurd for it is exhaustively explained as a necessary function of the mathematical postulates which make it possible. The root of the chestnut tree, or existence in general, cannot be thus explained for there exists no supreme geometer of being. Things simply *are* in a purely contingent, non-necessary way, which is maddening because they baffle the understanding: they are, as Roquentin puts it, *de trop* (the French means either "too much" or "importunate")—that is to say, rather like gate crashers at a party, imposing their presence upon unwilling guests who do not wish to be their accomplices or their witnesses. This fundamental absurdity of existence, its lack of justification, applies not only to mere things but to human existence; and it is the refusal to recognize this, the hiding behind self-important and self-justifying conventional social roles, which Roquentin/Sartre detests in the bourgeois of the Rue Tournebride or the portraits of the municipal museum. We will return to this scene in further detail shortly.

In the meantime the long-awaited rendezvous with Anny finally materializes. She and Roquentin realize that they have nothing further to say to each other beyond a tacit recognition that what they have in common is an existence that is desolate, entirely bereft of meaning. Both have renounced their former solutions for managing and neutralizing absurdity—"adventures" in the case of Roquentin and "perfect moments" or "privileged situations" in the case of Anny—but this common condition does not permit solidarity or complicity.

Sartre's intentions by this point are fairly clear: he has progressively foreclosed or eliminated the entire range of options to which most of us have recourse at some point or another as reasons for living: family, work, social success, romantic love, the "disinterested life of the mind," and so on. What Roquentin finally loses in this final encounter with Anny—and it should be borne in mind that since abandoning Rollebon he has lived only for this meeting with her—is not so much love as it is something more modest: companionship, or complicity, or at least a common understanding of a condition which is shared in the face of the absurd. Sartre is clearly concerned to reduce Roquentin to the purest and most extreme confrontation with what the author considers to be the authentic truth of our condition. And the implication is that this confrontation can only occur in a state of utter loneliness (rather than solitude, which is not the same thing and is rarely achieved in our modern urban conglomerates) and despair. Only in these circumstances, only in extremis, will Roquentin accede to the realization of his absurd and pointless freedom which Sartre considers to be the truth of the human condition:

> I'm free: I no longer have any reason to live, all those I've tried have given up on me and I cannot imagine any others. . . . The extent to which, at the height of my terrors, of my nauseas, I had counted on Anny to save me, I only now understand. My past is dead, M. de Rollebon is dead, Anny only came back in order to deprive me of all hope (N 156).

Roquentin's initial reaction to the discovery of his condition is despair. As he is about to leave Mudville for the last time, however, he listens one last time to "Some of These Days" and is, as usual, seduced by the mode of existence which it represents: a hard, pure, rigid necessity as opposed to the flaccid and absurd contingency of his own existence. He finally conceives of a form of salvation from his condition: producing a book which would acquire the aesthetic beauty of "Some of These Days" in the course of "making people ashamed of their existences" (N 178). This book is, of course, *Nausea* itself. By exposing and recounting the truth of nausea, of absurdity, he will be able to redeem its horrible stupid contingency by transforming it into art. So doing he will be able to turn his own life— although only as he contemplates it as a series of past events, not as he lives it (which will continue to be absurd and boring)—into something of an adventure, a novel:

> And there would be people who would read this novel and who would say, "It's Antoine Roquentin who wrote it, he was a red-headed guy who hung out in cafés," and they would think about my life in the same way I think about this black woman's life: as something precious and almost legendary ... Then perhaps I would be able to recall my life without repugnance. Perhaps one day, while thinking of this very moment, this dull moment when I am waiting, round-shouldered, for it to be time to get on the train, perhaps I would feel my heart beat faster and I would say to myself," It was that day at that moment that everything began." And I would manage—in the past, only in the past—to accept myself (N 178).

B. Historical Origins of the Absurd in the Modern West in the Commodification of All Being

In pursuit of our objective—"understanding Sartre," as our title would have it—it is necessary now to push our investigation beyond questions which can be answered by an examination of the formal structures of *Nausea*. Up to this point we have restricted ourselves to answering questions along the lines of Why does Roquentin consider music or "adventures," on the one hand, to be "hard," "rigorous," and exhilarating, and, on the other hand, normal existence as we live it and ordinary lived temporality to be absurd, "flabby," and generally disgusting? These questions can be answered at a first level by examining the novel on its own terms, as a totality like "Some of These Days" in which each element forms a meaningful part of a whole that is intentionally organized as a pattern of oppositions, resemblances, and differences and which strives to solicit a very specific aesthetic response on the part of the reader. (This conception of the work of art as a totality has been convincingly put in question by Marxist, psychoanalytic, and deconstructive literary critical theory. Indeed this conception—which we have ourselves adopted as a useful principle of organization for purposes of exposition in section A—identifies Sartre as squarely situated in that literary tradition known as *modernism*, which extends from the mid-nineteenth century (Baudelaire, Flaubert) down to roughly the end of the Second World War. For some consideration of the historical determinants and limitations of the notion of the work of art as a totality, see section C below.)

Clearly, however, if we are indeed to understand Sartre, we need also to put a different kind of question. Why, for example, does Sartre choose to present the contrast between art and existence in terms of the opposition between flabbiness and hardness? Or, more fundamentally, why does existence become *absurd* for so many writers of the period? We have mentioned that the latter phenomenon is related to the death of God; but why did God die? These are questions which transcend the formal organization of a novel and the aesthetic intentions of its author; and yet, they are crucial to an understanding of the most intimate details of the style and organization of the novel itself. Such considerations should not, in other words, take us away from the text to a domain which might somehow be construed as being "outside" of or even extraneous to it. We embark on an investigation of such questions only because it serves to illuminate the text.

We can begin with the question of the absurdity of existence and the inextricably related one of the death of God. In premodern societies all entities in the world, or universe, formed a cosmos—that is, as the Greek etymology of this word suggests, an order. Order in the cosmic sense of the term means more than the merely scientific order of cause and effect which we assume as the basis of our modern interpretations of the universe. Thus, modern science assumes, for example, the appearance of life on this planet and the gradual evolution of human beings and human societies to be no more than the product of chance, even if certain conditions necessarily have to be met before life can appear. In other words, the necessary combination of conditions for life to appear (including the universe itself) is a circumstance that is either attributed to chance or else ignored as something itself requiring explanation. In premodern cosmologies, however, such an event has its integral and functional place and explanation in a vital order which is intentionally organized, rather like a living organism, and which is ultimately sacred; and such is the place and function of all entities and all events.[2] Christianity as originally a premodern system of thought is one such cosmology: thus, we are told in the book of Genesis that before the creation there was "chaos," that is, an absence of such order. Dante, in the fourteenth century, himself already a transitional figure, would nonetheless express succinctly the Christian conception of the cosmos which dominated the Middle Ages. In his *Divine Comedy,* Beatrice explains to Dante:

> "All things," she said, "whatever they may be,
> Have order in themselves: this is the plan
> That makes the universe like unto God.
> It is herein that these exalted creatures
> Behold the imprint of the eternal power—
> The end for which this order was established.
> Within it, natural things are all disposed
> According to their several destinies,
> In varying nearness to their common source.
> Thence they issue forth to different havens
> Upon the mighty ocean of existence,
> Endowed each one with instinct to proceed.
> This instinct carries fire toward the moon;
> It is the motive force in mortal hearts;
> It binds together and unites the earth."[3]

Clearly there is no room for the Sartrean notion of the absurd in this kind of conception of existence.

To take another example that will be familiar to many readers, Shakespeare's *Macbeth* describes the assassination of the legitimate king of Scotland and the usurpation of his throne by Macbeth as a disturbance of an entire natural, divinely ordained order: the murder is accompanied by storms, earthquakes, unnatural acts on the part of animals. None of this "symbolizes"—as modern critics are tempted (anachronistically) to read the play today—the chaos unleashed in the political realm by the assassination: it *is* the chaos. This dimension of the play marks *Macbeth* as an invocation of the older medieval cosmic conception of the universe as a coherent moral order, a conception which is already on the way out at the time Shakespeare is writing.

A vivid sense of the change that has taken place since the time of Shakespeare can be gained by reflecting upon the fact that all that remains of Shakespeare's vestigially medieval cosmic order is the belief among Christians today that sin leads to hell and virtue to paradise. Shakespeare too believed this, but with a significant difference: the divine order of retribution to which Shakespeare subscribed operated *in this life* as well as in the hereafter. (Many Christians believe this today, but all too often in a simple-minded manner, with little of the understanding that Shakespeare has of the notion of divine retribution emanating from a cosmic law, something which is in the very nature of things as a law of life having the kind of force that gravity and death have.) This is powerfully exemplified in the career of Macbeth himself, as his crimes inexorably isolate him from those around him, culminating in a condition of complete aloneness-in-the-world in which he concludes that "Life ... is a tale / Told by an idiot, full of sound and fury, / Signifying nothing." Evil, in other words, makes life worthless, a living hell. Modern Christianity has generally either restricted the meaning and consequences of behavior to the afterlife (one is consigned to heaven or hell according to one's record), or, in the tradition which has sprung out of Luther, salvation is deemed to depend upon faith alone. In both cases neither God nor a divine order is operative in the world in which we live; there is no understanding of the *material consequences* of good and evil, whereas Shakespeare demonstrates Macbeth consigning himself to hell *on earth* because of the kind of person he has to become in order to perform his monstrous acts. Shakespeare is able to achieve this—and this is the condition of the enduring greatness of the play—because he is able to draw on a worldview which apprehends each human action as one which has repercussions for the entire cosmos. A moment's reflection should make it apparent that in this respect Shakespeare's religious beliefs, like those of most traditional premodern societies, were in fact much more *scientific* than our average mainstream contemporary Christianity which, with notable exceptions (for example, contemporary liberation theology in Latin America), carefully avoids the question of the material effects of human activity and emphasizes intead blind Faith or the consequences of vice and virtue for the afterlife. We are, contrary to the complacent view which modernity has of itself, far more irrational, "primitive," and superstitious than most other societies on historical record. Modern Christians are often rigorous atheists with respect to this world of material objects and flesh and blood, and primitive cult worshipers with respect to everything else. This is precisely what Nietzsche announced with "the death of God" and "the advent of nihilism." Whereas God, or the gods, had once—in animism, for example, but even vestigially in Christianity in the doctrine of the transubstantiation of the Eucharist—been an integral immanent part of this world, in modernity (since the Renaissance) the divine has progessively retreated into a transcendental heaven which is as remote as the world left behind is meaningless.[4]

By the time Sartre is writing, this development has reached its culmination, and *Nausea* is a response to this historically novel situation: it is both a registering of this state of affairs and an attempt to deal with it: "Where do we go from now?"

The question which we have to answer here is, How did all of this happen? What was the cause of the death of God and the transformation of the world into a meaningless absurdity?

Meaninglessness is by common agreement a product of the modern world—that is to say, the world which has come into being since the rise of capitalism beginning at the end of the Middle Ages and the appearance of its indispensable instrument and product, modern science. Thus, for example, the massive urbanization and organization of work in factories which this eventually entailed, we are told, led to the destruction of traditional family structures (for example, an extended family living under one roof or in one settlement) and belief systems which had made sense of hunter-gatherer or agricultural modes of existence in earlier periods. Most importantly, modern science, receiving a tremendous impulse from a constant capitalist demand for innovation (in order to lower costs by increasing productivity)—(a primitive steam engine had been used in ancient Egypt, for example, but the social conditions for its widespread implementation did not exist: i.e. the *economy* could not make use of it)—penetrating and accounting for more and more domains of existence in a manner which permitted *material control* of these domains, dispelled religious belief and doctrine with its demonstrably more powerful and cogent explanations, discrediting countless religious texts and beliefs.

This is all doubtless true. But it is, at this stage, far too vague for our purposes. After all, Sartre is quite specific: in *Nausea,* ordinary objects of the most banal kind are being perceived in a new and disturbing manner. What does all the above have to do with *belief*? One might begin, quite rightly, by pointing out that beliefs are not merely intellectual matters and that a religious worldview entails consequences at the level of perception. But what we really need is to demonstrate how the perception of ordinary everyday objects has changed since the Middle Ages and the onset of the Renaissance, culminating in Sartre's disgusting chestnut tree.

The great historians of the Middle Ages suggest that in that period ordinary objects were regularly perceived as having religious significance. Huizinga gives the example of the humble walnut: "the sweet kernel is His divine nature, the green and pulpy outer peel is His humanity, the wooden shell between is the cross."[5] To take another example, in the medieval French epic *The Song of Roland,* when the hero is about to die after having fought a Saracen army to a standstill, his final moments are described in the following manner: "Roland feels that his death is drawing close ... He mounts a small knoll. There, under two handsome trees, there are four marble steps. On the green grass he has fallen on his back. He swoons, for his death approaches."[6] Given certain other pointers in the story (such as the fact that the rearguard of the French army is protected by Roland and twelve other knights, which recalls Christ's apostles, and that Roland and his companions are betrayed by a Judaslike character called Ganelon), the details of this little scene (the small knoll upon which Roland expires flanked by two trees, having surmounted marble steps [a sign of royal power in the period]) induce the Christian reader to perceive Roland's death as a replay of the crucifixion of Christ, "King of the Jews."

Nothing could resemble less these two medieval trees, which are simultaneously the crosses of the two thieves flanking Christ at Golgotha, than the absurd chestnut tree in *Nausea,* which is not only bereft of the power to symbolize something other than itself but has almost lost the power to vibrate to the concepts which we normally use to denote it:

> The root of the chestnut buried itself in the earth, just below my bench. I no longer remembered that it was a root. Words had melted away and, with them, the meaning of things, the ways in which we use them, the feeble points of reference which men have traced on their surface (N 126–127).

But how did we reach this state of affairs?

The modern age is correctly described as being above

all characterized by change. Which is not to say that premodern societies did not change and evolve. They did, sometimes catastrophically. What distinguishes modern society from any other is that change is built into it as its very essence or inner dynamic. Modern society, in other words, could not survive *without* change. This is easily demonstrated: if all Americans were suddenly to decide to wear out all their consumer goods before replacing them, the country (and the world at large) would instantly be plunged into a major economic crisis. The mechanisms that prevent us from meeting this dire fate are changes in fashion and the advertisement industries which promote them. There is a constant attempt to persuade us that what we already have, and which still perfectly serves the purpose for which it was purchased, should be replaced by something that is more attractive and more prestigious because it is newer and more fashionable. This attempt is endlessly repeated, and successfully so. This is familiar to all of us and might not warrant much comment here were it not for the profound transformation it entails in our relations not only with consumer objects but with the totality of being.

We can examine this transformation and its consequences in a moment. In the meantime, it must be emphasized that what we call "fashion" is but one dimension of a vaster project of permanent transformation of modern society as a whole which is demanded by the dynamic of an advanced capitalist economy (we do not have space here to trace these changes from the first appearance of capitalism at the end of the medieval period, and so must restrict ourselves to the industrial capitalism of the nineteenth and twentieth centuries). In order to survive, all capitalists competing for the same market have to sell their product for at least the same price as their major competitors are selling it. Ideally they would like to cut the price still further in order to obtain an even bigger slice of the market. This fact places all capitalists under immense and constant pressure to reduce the costs of production. Failing an increase in the motivation of their workers to work harder for the same wages (which is improbable), the most obvious solution is newer machinery which produces more products in the same period of time and with less worker participation. This fact is the most important single reason for the advances we have made in science over the last few centuries. New technology, however, always entails the transformation of the society's major institutions because the new technology cannot be used without these changes. For example, the introduction of factories during the Industrial Revolution probably did more than anything else to destroy what was left of the extended family because it took work out of the household in order to organize it more strictly and productively.

In short, a constantly changing and evolving society produces constantly changing institutions and the new kinds of *people* who are functionally adapted to them, with new values and new sensibilities occurring in as little as a single generation. (The "generation gap" with its distinctive conflictual parent-child relations is one consequence of this process and is found much more often, and in acuter forms, in modern society than in any other we know.)

Once this process of constant transformation is taking place with sufficient rapidity for the participants to become aware of the fact, cultural and historical relativity become a part of collective awareness. (This is the principal reason both for the appearance of academic history in its familiar modern shape and a demand for historical verisimilitude in historical fiction, whereas Shakespeare's contemporaries had no problem with performing *Julius Caesar* in Elizabethan dress.) Now, it is easy to understand how this process might contribute to the erosion of all traditional values, including the death of God; but it does not quite suffice to explain why objects should come to acquire the kind of baffling, enigmatic quality of just stupidly and absurdly *being-there* which they have in *Nausea*. As an entire society undergoes constant and fundamental change, so the objects that society relates to change in meaning: thoroughly mediocre pieces of furniture which could only have graced the room of a maidservant in the eighteenth century are sold today as prized antiques; nature itself is no longer the same—we have never been so effusive about nature as we are today now that we are poised on the brink of destroying the entire ecosystem. This phenomenon of the constant restless change in the meaning and identity of entities—most obviously manifested at the level of fashion, but applying to everything under advanced capitalism, including people—eventually leads to the lowest common denominator of all entities emerging as a new conceptual acquisition of the society or civilization in question: existence. Is-ness.

Furthermore, because constant social transformation has effectively killed God (whatever people's *beliefs* in this regard, which are, strictly speaking, irrelevant because it is in our *relation to the world* that

70

the modern West has become atheistic), the confrontation with the lowest common denominational is-ness takes the form of a bewildered musing Why is there something, rather than nothing? To which, of course, under these prevailing circumstances, there is no answer.

C. The Modernist Aesthetic—the Work of Art as Totality—as Redemption of the Absurd, Substitute for the Divine in a Fallen World, Mirror-image of the Commodity Form, and Purveyor of the Gender Ideology of the Bourgeois Nuclear Family

We are now in a position to understand why it is that Sartre/Roquentin deems art to offer a solution—albeit a limited one (see the conclusion to section A above)—to the problem of living in an absurd world. To the extent that the successful work of art of the modernist aesthetic, as we have seen, presents itself as a perfect totality (a claim which deconstructive and Marxist criticism will subsequently challenge) in which all its aspects exist in relations of internal necessity with one another—thereby making them all *meaningful* in terms of one another—it enables itself to stand as an imaginary utopian redemption of meaninglessness in the world.[7] It reproduces, in other words, in secularized, humanized, form the divinely ordered cosmos of premodern societies the characteristics of which we examined in the preceding section. In short, the modern artist replaces God as creator in an existential move that consecrates the death of God, which would have been conceived as blasphemous in an earlier age,

71

and that exactly parallels the drive of the modern scientist or capitalist to be sole legislator and artificer of a humanized and technologically tamed (commodified) world of purely rational and material relations. (This move also involves inextricably related secret complicities with an entire gender ideology as we shall see shortly.)

Art, as a social activity radically distinct from the domains of religious ritual and economic production, of which it was formerly, in most cases, an integral part (as, for example, in the case of medieval cathedrals, or the ordinary utensils and weapons of everyday life), employing its specialized autonomous full-time practitioners, is with few exceptions really a product of modernity. It is clear now why this should have been so. It would also seem to be a strong probability—now that as of the 1950s, we have reached the end of modernity and have passed into "postmodernity"—that we will see the end of art as we have known it. If we survive the ecological catastrophe currently facing us, it will only be on the basis of the kind of practical *material* understanding of the sacredness of the entire life system of the planet evinced in Chief Seattle's letter quoted in note 4. The great art works of the future, and inevitably our social arrangements, will reflect this in a new synthesis of "science" and "religion" as cosmic law—a synthesis which will be as much "material" as "spiritual" (a false distinction which achieves its most destructive manifestations in Western modernity, and of which Sartre's work is a glaring example). Indeed, this is already happening, as the remarkable novels of Michel Tournier demonstrate (see especially *Friday,* in which just such a cosmic aesthetic is explicitly formulated; see also the work of Ursula Le Guin).

Sartre is far from being the originator of the conception of art as redeemer of the death of God which he merely brings to its apotheosis. Kant laid the groundwork for it:

> The judgement of taste can be determined by no representation of an objective purpose, i.e. of the possibility of the object itself in accordance with principles of purposive combination, and consequently by no concept of good .... It therefore has to do with no concept of the character and internal or external possibility of the object by means of this or that cause, *but merely with the relation of the representative powers to one another,* so far as they are determined by a representation.[8]

The work of art, in other words, is not "good for something"—an instrument which can be used toward an end extraneous to itself—but "good in itself," a perfected totality, like the divine creation, in which all its components (the "representative powers") are in harmonious relation to one another such that the work stands aloof from the fallen world of busy and grubby, meaningless, vulgar practical activity. This is the secret consolation of art in the modern age. This is its "beauty." (Significantly, as we shall see, Sartre will move away from what is essentially still a Kantian conception of art in *Nausea* to a politically "engaged" notion of art in the later works.)

Now, we have attempted to provide an answer to the question as to why existence and its meaninglessness becomes a central preoccupation of the writers of the period in which *Nausea* was written. We have suggested that the reasons lie in a culmination of long-term historical processes beginning in the Renaissance, rather than in more immediate and historically local causes such as the catastrophe of World War I, or the economic crises of the 20s and 30s, to which so much literary experiment of the period is traditionally linked in literary histories. War and economic crisis—scarcely novelties in human history, after all—only underscore in dramatic fashion the meaninglessness of existence if the latter is already so as a broad cultural phenomenon. (In the "age of faith," for example, these kinds of catastrophes generally led to excesses of religious mania rather than crises of belief).

We have still to explain why the absurdity of existence should provoke *disgust,* nausea. Why not mere despair, for example? Why this visceral reaction?[9]

We can begin attempting to answer this question by recalling the other "extratextual" question we raised at the outset of section B above: Why does Roquentin consider music or "adventures" to be "hard," "rigorous," and exhilarating, and, ordinary existence as we normally live it to be "flabby"? Why does Sartre set up the opposition in these terms? The following passage from the first description of Roquentin's enjoyment of "Some of These Days" gives us a good indication:

> What has just happened is that the Nausea has disappeared. When the voice rose, in the silence, I felt my body harden and the Nausea melted away. It happened all in one go: it was almost painful to become all hard like that, a brilliant burning red. At the same time the music was drawn out, it swelled like a waterspout (N 22).

One does not have to be a committed Freudian to be alive to the sexual dimension of this passage: the deliberate collocation of the description of the male listener's body hardening and stiffening to the music with the account of the music as swelling and dilating is the most obvious instance of the constant assimilation in *Nausea* of music or art to a male erection. This equivalence is consistently reinforced by the description of that with which art is contrasted in the novel: thus, existence is regularly associated with what our culture classifies as femininity. On two occasions in the central scene in the park Roquentin, while grasping for the terms in which to describe his understanding of the absurd, has recourse to similes or recollections involving women in order more precisely to define his experience of the "monstrous, flabby, disorderly masses [of existence]—naked, of a frightening and obscene nudity" (N 127). In one of these comparisons he recalls the breasts of the woman who had been at the *Brasserie Vezelise* as a case of "naked existence" which it "gives him a turn" to think of as continuing to exist (N 134). When existence, as that which is opposed in the novel to art (or mathematics), is not being denigrated as feminine and thereby disgusting or obscene, it is assimilated to failed virility: thus, Roquentin expects the trees in the municipal park at any instant to "become wrinkled like tired penises, to shrivel up and fall to the ground" (N 133; Alexander translates the French *verges* as "wands"—one possible sense of the word in French but which is not convincing in the context).

It is no accident that existence at its most absurd and most repulsive is evoked in the form of organic nature. The oppression of women by men has been either a permanent feature of social organization or one of very long duration (the question does not seem to have been settled decisively by feminist scholarship), and while there have been transhistorical constants in this oppression it has also displayed features that are specific to each period and culture. The form of misogyny we find apparent in *Nausea*—that is, the assimilation of woman to nature and vice versa, an equivalence in which both poles evoke intense disgust (as in the chestnut tree scene, but more obviously in the important dream Roquentin has while in the arms of the owner of the Rendezvous des Cheminots where he assimilates the woman's genitalia to a park full of revolting nightmarish insects (N 59)—this kind of misogyny, although it has some antecedents in earlier periods, is most powerfully and insistently expressed in the period of industrial capitalism: 1) Nature, as we have seen, only really becomes meaningless—something which can be ruthlessly exploited and damaged with impunity (we are not a part of it and it is not a part of us)—in modernity because capitalism could not expand and develop without this assumption. (Under the pressure of the collapse of the environment which is currently threatening our very survival—a direct consequence of this attitude—we are now groping toward alternative attitudes toward nature.) 2) In the eyes of the post-Renaissance humanism which has dominated Western thought until very recently, "man" was the measure of the world, of meaning (rather than the old cosmic order). This tacitly assumed that nature was meaningless (i.e., not a meaningfully organized totality). When, under the variety of industrial capitalism which rested upon the nuclear family, women were confined to the role of childbearers and domestic workers who were not ostensibly engaged in economic activity because they did not earn a wage and because they did not transform matter into commodities (although, of course, their work was in fact crucial to the economy), it was easy to establish an equivalence between meaningless nature and women as merely passive creatures abandoning themselves to their purely contingent biological natures as reproducing machines. Just as, in terms of the same oppositions, it was easy to establish that any totality—a work of art, or simply any commodity (this is in fact what is really at stake here)—must be the product of the activity of an imperial, masculine, godlike subject whose project penetrated and completely informed otherwise meaningless feminine matter.

These hidden assumptions are fundamental to Sartre's writing at this stage of his career and have been inherited from the tradition of modernism to which he is an heir. Thus, there is a clear affinity between Sartre's desire to deny the (for him) repulsive human body and accede to pure thought (as in the Boulevard Noir passage) and the whole tradition which runs from French Symbolism (Baudelaire, Rimbaud, Mallarmé, et al.) down to Proust and Sartre in which the human creation or fictional world—the *image*—is deemed superior to the fallen, contingent, natural *given,* mere *thing,* or mere *life.* Proust, for example (whose influence Sartre freely recognized), maintained that the novelist's "decisive perfection" of life consisted in the suppression of real characters which were "impenetrable" to the "total notion" of the artist and their replacement by an "image" which was "the only essential element."[10]

Thus we see that the modernist artwork like *Nausea* performs a number of interrelated social functions: 1) it replaces the dead deity; 2) while decrying the vulgar practical commercial activity of everyday bourgeois life which is hopelessly alienated to the production of wealth (whereas the work of art presents itself as an end in itself) it nonetheless ultimately buys into the thoroughly bourgeois-capitalist notion of the superiority of the human totality (i.e. commodity) as a transformation of contingent natural matter; 3) it reinforces the industrial-capitalist functionally necessary institution of the nuclear family with its division of labor between the male wage-earner who participates in the transformation of matter and the female domestic drudge who is irrevocably assigned to the realm of contingent natural reproduction and nurturance.

In this respect *Nausea* can be said to have contributed, at a subliminal level, to the maintaining of women in "their place." This is "unconscious" on Sartre's part in the sense that, even if there is clearly a visceral complicity on his part with the broad cultural discourse of misogyny he is drawing upon, like all of us he is not aware at the time of writing of the ultimate political-economic consequences of what he is doing. Furthermore, Sartre's subsequent writings give proof of an evolution toward a much more positive attitude toward women and "femininity" and an implicit critique of the earlier positions developed in *Nausea*. And there is, of course, his subsequent support of the work of his feminist companion and lover, Simone de Beauvoir.

Finally, the ambivalence in Sartre's representation of woman and nature must be emphasized. After all, the feminine, contingent, nauseating absurd is presented as an authentic truth which conventional bourgeois society refuses to acknowledge—even if Roquentin (like Sartre himself) in the final analysis can only deal with the absurd by neutralizing it in the course of transforming it into a reassuringly necessary (and thereby, according to the terms of the book, masculine) aesthetic enterprise.[11]

Sartre's attitude toward women is all the more ambivalent and contradictory to the extent that while on the one hand, as we have seen, some strands of his writing implicitly endorse the nuclear-familial stereotype of the woman as mere biological housewife-incubator, others anticipate more recent arrangements of the postnuclear family. Roquentin's own life style is in fact perfectly adapted to our contemporary services economy where the domestic labor formerly performed by women (who are now no longer available for such labor) has been industrialized and is sold to workers as consumer products—fast food, for example. Thus Roquentin (like Sartre himself) lives out of cheap hotels, restaurants, and cafés. Furthermore, he is clearly hostile to marriage and has a love life which, in its degree of freedom, would only become universally available to the middle classes in the 60s. (Indeed, Sartre, like the other great modernist writers of the twentieth century, is in part responsible for the explosive demand for such freedoms in the 1960s). There is hardly any room for the oppressed wife of the nuclear family in any of this.[12]

NOTES

1. When I say that the novel is being read in this section "on its own terms" this is not intended to suggest that we are thereby acceding to some geniunely "objective" existence of the text or the author's "intentions" before the interpretative intervention of a historically situated reader or critic. Rather, this is merely an abbreviated way of saying that I am laying out the systems of binary oppositions thanks to which the novel is able to function as an aesthetic artifact and of which Sartre himself may well not be the master. It is simply easier to do this for purposes of clear exposition and explanation before proceeding to the explicitly critical examination of these oppositions in sections B and C of this chapter. That we are ourselves in large measure still enmeshed in the oppositions that Sartre mobilizes (despite the dated character of the novel), and that our ostensibly "uncritical" unpacking of their structure is itself directed by an agenda, goes without saying.

2. Interestingly enough, contemporary science is starting to recognize that assumptions along these lines may well be necessary for modern science itself to accomplish its mission. Thus, the remarkable work of James Lovelock—on the processes whereby the composition of the earth's atmosphere has been carefully regulated by the sum total of all organisms on the planet in such a manner as to sustain life—suggests that life on earth is a self-regulating process or single organism in which all living species are vital components, like the individual cells of a body (James Lovelock, *The Ages of Gaia: a Biography of Our Living Earth* [New York: Norton, 1988]).

3. Dante Alighieri, *The Divine Comedy,* trans. Lawrence Grant White (New York: Pantheon, 1958), 130.

4. For a more extended account of this historical process see my forthcoming *From Existentialism to Poststructuralism and the Coming of the Postindustrial Age* (Stanford University Press, 1991). The fatal consequence of this reduction of Being to meaninglessness, this loss of the sense of Being as sacred (a loss which is already immanent in Christianity itself with its inherent Platonism—Being is only sacred to the extent that it points to another realm [rather than being sacred *in its own right*], the divine, which is *separate* and distinct from our own), is that the way is wide open to the reckless assault on the planetary ecosystem which now threatens us with extinction.

Our modern Western "civilization," of which we are accustomed to be so insufferably proud, and in the name of which we have consistently represented ourselves as superior to all other ages and cultures, cannot be judged in these circumstances as anything other than the worst and most criminal barbarism ever to have emerged on the face of the planet (a barbarism of which *Nausea* is the highest artistic expression). For a marvelous and compelling corrective to our Western mindset, I know of none better than the letter Chief Seattle wrote to the President of the United States in 1852:

"The President in Washington sends word that he wishes to buy our land. But how can you buy or sell the sky? The land? The idea is strange to us. If you do not own the freshness of the air and the sparkle of the water, how can you buy them?

"Every part of this earth is sacred to my people. Every shining pine needle, every sandy shore, every mist in the dark woods, every meadow, every humming insect. All are holy in the memory and experience of my people. . . .

"This we know: the earth does not belong to man, man belongs to the earth. All things are connected like the blood that unites us all. Man did not weave the web of life, he is merely a strand in it. Whatever he does to the web, he does to himself. . . .

"Your destiny is a mystery to us. What will happen when the buffalo are all slaughtered? The wild horses tamed? What will happen when the secret corners of the forest are heavy with the scent of many men and the view of the ripe hills is blotted by talking wires? Where will the thicket be? Gone! Where will the eagle be? Gone! And what is it to say goodbye to the swift pony and the hunt? The end of living and the beginning of survival" (quoted in Joseph Campbell, *The Power of Myth* [Garden City, NY. Doubleday, 1988]), 34).

5. Johan Huizinga, *The Waning of the Middle Ages* (Garden City, NY: Doubleday Anchor Books, 1954) 206.

6. *The Song of Roland,* v. 2259–70; my translation.

7. The notion of the work of art as a perfected totality is a constant theme of aesthetic meditation by the great modernists (of which Sartre is one of the last representatives). Thus, at the beginning of the modernist period, Baudelaire expresses the notion particularly well: "In the entire composition not a single word must slip in which

is not an intention, which does not tend, directly or indirectly, to perfect the premeditated plan" (Charles Baudelaire, "Notes nouvelles sur E. A. Poe," *Nouvelles Histoires extraordinaires* [Paris: Conard, 1933], p. xii). See also Paul Valéry, *Oeuvres*, vol. 1, Bibliothèque de la Pléiade (Paris: Gallimard, 1957) 1786.

8. Quoted in Harzard Adams, ed., *Critical Theory since Plato* (New York: Harcourt, Brace, 1971) 384.

9. The reader interested in pursuing this issue should see Serge Doubrovsky's two fine essays: "Phallotexte et gynotexte dans *La Nausée:* 'Feuillet sans date,'" *Sartre et la mise en signe,* ed. Michael Issacharoff and Jean-Claude Vilquin (Lexington, KY: French Forum Monographs, 1982), and "Le Neuf de Coeur: Fragment d'une psycholecture de *La Nausée,*" *Obliques,* 18–19 (1979): 67–73.

10. Marcel Proust, *A la recherche du temps perdu,* vol. 1, Bibliothèque de la Pléiade (Paris: Gallimard, 1954) 88.

11. It has to be said, however, that even this maneuver ultimately consigns women to their traditional place within the classical Freudian (and therefore patriarchal) schema in which woman is the representative of truth (i.e. as nudity, as in *Nausea*) and therefore of castration anxiety. Hence the powerful reaction of disgust in the face of the "obscene nudity" of the absurd on the part of Sartre/Roquentin. See the third part of Jacques Derrida's *The Postcard: From Socrates to Freud and Beyond,* trans. Alan Bass (Chicago: University of Chicago Press, 1987); also available as "The Purveyor of Truth," *Yale French Studies* 52 (1975): 31–114.

12. Although, of course, there may well be room for sexual oppression in the new arrangements (this was precisely the charge feminists leveled at the concept of "liberated" sexuality entertained by many members of the New Left in the 60s). See, e.g., Suzanne Lilar's critical account of the relationship between Sartre and Simone de Beauvoir, *Le Malentendu du deuxième sexe* (Paris: P.U.F., 1967).

CHAPTER THREE

Roads to Freedom: The Age of Reason; The Reprieve; Troubled Sleep

The constant concern of Sartre's literary production from 1940 down to his last great play twenty years later, *The Condemned of Altona,* is the predicament of the lone individual confronted with history as a massive, ineluctable challenge to freedom and responsibility. Simone de Beauvoir has described in her autobiography the important change she noticed had come over Sartre when he returned from his experience, first as a soldier and then as a prisoner of war, of the catastrophic defeat of France at the hands of Nazi Germany in 1940. World history had become an inescapable "situation" in which the individual was condemned to make fundamental choices which were always, in the final analysis, of a broadly social and political import. Even an abstention from social involvement was a political choice insofar as one was thereby making the progress of political oppression easier.

This new political awareness on the part of Sartre is what radically distinguishes the post–1940 writings from *Nausea.* Roquentin was, at least in terms of the narrow conventional understanding of "politics," fiercely apolitical. While it is clear that he detests the ruling classes of the French Third Republic, the idea of him joining, say, the French Communist Party or enlisting on either side of the Spanish Civil War would be inconceivable.[1] Again, Simone de Beauvoir described how, before the war, both she and Sartre were sympathetic to broadly left-wing causes—they supported the Left coalition of the *Front Populaire,* for example—but nevertheless did not feel that such issues directly concerned them. They felt themselves to be detached observers. From 1940 onward this would change fundamentally: Orestes in *The Flies,* Mathieu Delarue in *Roads to Freedom,* Hugo Barine in *Dirty Hands,* Goetz in *The Devil and the Good Lord,* Frantz von Gerlach in *The Condemned of Altona*—all these central characters from the bulk of Sartre's writing over this period of some twenty years constitute urgent and anguished explorations of this new situation in which far from being meaningless or absurd, as in *Nausea,* the world has on the contrary become charged with a threatening historical meaning which one necessarily engages with in one way or another.

I. Understanding the Novel on Its Own Terms

A. Freedom, Responsibility, the Individual and World History

The main character of the incomplete *Roads to Freedom,*[2] Mathieu Delarue, stands as Sartre's most extended treatment of his new problem. The first volume of the trilogy, *The Age of Reason,* opens in the spring of 1938 and turns round the fact that Mathieu, a thirty-four old teacher of philosophy in the French equivalent of a public high school, has got his lover of seven years, Marcelle, pregnant. Mathieu, like the young Sartre himself, is obsessed with being the author of his own life, with making all the dimensions of his existence stem solely from his untrammeled personal choice. For example, when his best friend, the communist militant and journalist Brunet, urges him to join the French Communist Party, he declares that while he supports the party's cause and can think of no reason why he should *not* join, he nonetheless cannot do so because he can find no compelling reasons *of his own* for doing so. He and Marcelle have never married because they consider marriage to be bourgeois servitude; and they have a long-standing agreement that in the event of her becoming pregnant they will have recourse to abortion. At the time, however, abortion is still illegal and thus very expensive if performed by a qualified doctor. Mathieu tries unsuccessfully to borrow the money from the only two sources available to him, his elder brother, Jacques, and a friend, Daniel. The situation is complicated by the fact that although he still has esteem and affection for Marcelle, Mathieu is no longer in love with her. Their relationship had always been open-ended (he has Marcelle's permission to pursue other women while remaining her lover), and he is presently obsessed by a much younger woman of twenty-one, Ivich. In the meantime, unbeknownst to Mathieu, Marcelle secretly wants the child but has not felt up to telling him this. While she feels constrained by their agreement, she nonetheless resents its not having even occurred to Mathieu to ask her whether she might want to keep the child.

Furthermore, Mathieu's friend Daniel, an embittered closet homosexual who has internalized the conventional fear and loathing of homosexuality and for this reason cannot accept his own sexuality, secretly detests what he erroneously takes to be Mathieu's untormented "normal" existence. He decides through sheer spite to try and ruin Mathieu's life by manipulating the situation in order to oblige Mathieu to marry the woman he no longer loves. He pretends not to have the money Mathieu needs and persuades Marcelle that she is right to want to keep the child—he can suggest obliquely to Mathieu that for all he knows this may indeed be Marcelle's desire. He proceeds to do this and then, after meeting with Mathieu, insinuates mendaciously to Marcelle that his parting impression of Mathieu's intentions was that the latter had already suspected Marcelle's secret desire to have the child and was now remorseful and ready to make reparations. Mathieu, however, still dreads having to marry Marcelle under duress; unable or unwilling to abandon her frankly and brutally, he seizes upon an unexpected opportunity to steal the money for the abortion from an acquaintance, with the intention of paying it back at a later date.

Two days after their meeting at the beginning of the book Mathieu returns to Marcelle with the money. He admits to having stolen it whereupon she understands the intensity of his desire not to have the child and not to be committed to her. At this point, as a feeble gesture to his sense of duty—precisely when her pride will understandably make such a proposition unacceptable because she now has to face the fact that he no longer loves her—Mathieu rather halfheartedly raises the possibility of their getting married. She refuses and tells him that he no longer loves her. He admits this, but still tries foolishly and spinelessly— because he cannot face the sense of guilt entailed by his own desires and actions—to save what has become an irreparable situation. She flings the money in his face and throws him out. Mathieu returns to his apartment to find Ivich—whom he has continued to court assiduously during the two days he has been trying to raise the money for Marcelle's abortion—and fails in a final attempt to seduce her. Alone in his apartment that evening, realizing that he has abandoned Marcelle "for nothing" (AR 371), he is visited by Daniel, who reveals to him for the first time that he is a homosexual and that Marcelle has just accepted his proposal of marriage. The book concludes with this crushing culmination to what Mathieu has been slowly learning over the previous two days—that his vaunted individualistic "freedom" was merely futile egotistical irresponsibility.

The Age of Reason can only really be understood as a part of the trilogy as a whole, and so we should take a brief look at the two later volumes before returning to all of this in detail. *The Reprieve* takes up the lives of the main characters six months later during the week of the great European political crisis provoked by Hitler's territorial demands on Czechoslovakia in the fall of 1938. The crisis was only resolved by the capitulation of the protectors of Czechoslovakian territorial integrity and sovereignty—France and Great Britain—in the Munich accord which effectively led to German dismemberment and then absorption of Czechoslovakia. Sartre introduces a host of new, minor, characters, and the narrative constantly jumps back and forth without warning between their lives and those of the main characters and the various historical personages involved in the negotiations concerning the political crisis—Hitler, Chamberlain, the French leader (Daladier). Sartre's intention was clearly to weave a tapestry of a wide range of characters from all walks of life who frequently do not know one another, and who often never meet, in order to convey a sense of the great historical drama as one immensely complex event in which all the concerned millions of the various populations are inescapably involved.

As one part of its response to Hitler's demands France mobilizes part of its reserves of civilian conscripts, including Mathieu, who is still trying to assimilate the meaninglessness of his life up to this point. We observe his attempts to deal with the awakening understanding—thrust upon him for the first time by the nature of the political crisis and his mobilization, an understanding which could not be available to him for as long as he saw himself as an extrasocial or private individual, nothing more than a schoolteacher, Marcelle's lover, Daniel's friend, and so on —that he is ineluctably caught up in a vast historical process which vitally concerns the entire planet, including himself. The immediate crisis is, finally, defused by the agreement reached at Munich and Mathieu is demobilized for another year, believing that the whole event would be without further consequences. He is no longer the same man, however.

The action of *Troubled Sleep*[3] takes place during a few days in June 1940 immediately after the surrender of France. The novel falls into two sections. The bulk of the first half is devoted to portraying Mathieu's assimilation of the ignominious rout of the French army, which has rendered the national drama in which he has just been caught up as shameful and futile as his own civilian life. Depressed by the demoralization around him—his unit hasn't even seen the enemy, let alone fired a shot; they have been abandoned by their officers, and drunkenness has broken out among the troops—and feeling that he has lived to absolutely no avail, he joins on an impulse a small handful of die-hards from another unit who have decided to fight to the finish despite the armistice that has just been proclaimed. In this last, suicidal gesture, he attempts desperately to redeem the nullity of his existence by at least *choosing* to die "for nothing" (TS 228), as he puts it, instead of drifting halfheartedly through the nothingness of his existence. He will have at least chosen his futile destiny. We last see him firing furiously on German troops from a church tower.

The second half of *Troubled Sleep* is devoted to Mathieu's friend, the communist militant Brunet, who has fought in the front lines and is now in a prison-camp. The important thing about this character is that he has clearly been created as a foil to Mathieu: we see him undergoing an evolution in the opposite direction of that undertaken by his friend. In the course of being constantly challenged by a mysterious fellow prisoner called Schneider, he progresses from being the diametrical contrary of Mathieu—a rather tediously rigid and doctrinaire militant whose greatest weakness is an almost religious faith in the Marxist laws of history (and what Sartre portrays critically as a correspondingly underdeveloped faith in human beings)—to an increasing sense of the complexity and provisional character of thought and reality.

At this point the trilogy ends. From what can be gleaned from the incomplete fourth volume of the novel, *The Last Chance,* and Simone de Beauvoir's summary of Sartre's intentions for this final volume, it appears that Schneider is really one Vicarios, also a journalist, who had left the Communist Party as a protest against the pact of nonaggression between the Soviet Union and Germany, which had given Hitler a free hand in the West and spared the Germans their traditional fear of a war on two fronts. The party had then denounced Vicarios as a police informer in order to disqualify the criticism entailed in his resignation. Disgusted by this calumny, Brunet for the first time has to put the party's policies and dogma in question and mobilize his own judgment. He escapes from the camp, successfully rehabilitates Vicarios/Schneider, and continues his activity as a committed communist militant in the French Resistance without renouncing his newly won independence of thought. Mathieu, who has survived his last stand, has by now renounced being a free-floating intellectual paralyzed by introspective speculation, free "for nothing," and has come to a similar position of commitment from the opposite direction, being similarly actively engaged in the Resistance. He eventually dies heroically under torture at the hands of the Germans. The resolution of the antithetical opposition between the two men in a new symmetrical synthesis points to Sartre's ideal: existential freedom which is responsibly engaged, committed in the political struggle but which is nonetheless always *problematic,* not dogmatic, and always ready to put itself in question as its own sole ultimate court of appeal.

Now that we have some idea of Sartre's overall aesthetic project in this large and sprawling novel, we can undertake a more detailed analysis that will enable us both to understand this aesthetic project on its own terms and to explain how and why a work of this kind should have come into being at this point in history and what its broad historical or cultural significance really is. Ideally, these two accounts should complement each other.

The principal theme of the trilogy is announced in the opening pages of *The Age of Reason*. Mathieu is on his way to the fateful meeting with Marcelle, where she announces her pregnancy, when he is accosted by a drunk who, after Mathieu has given him some money, shows him a stamped envelope from Spain and blurts out in a sudden access of passion that he had wanted to go to Spain to take part in the civil war but that somehow it had not worked out. As Mathieu takes leave of him, the drunk offers to stand Mathieu to a drink. The latter tactfully declines and continues on his way, reflecting regretfully that there had been a time when he would have accepted such an improbable invitation. "I'm getting old," he concludes (AR 5).

The opposition between youth and adulthood (the "age of reason" of the title) is the most obvious theme of the first volume of the trilogy and is inextricably bound up with the central preoccupation of the entire work: individual freedom confronted by its inescapable responsibility not only to those in our immediate entourage but to all humanity as players in one vast historical drama in which all our actions have consequences for all the participants. The stage is set in this opening of the first chapter, for when Mathieu gets to Marcelle's room he recounts to her his meeting with the drunk as well as the vague regret he had felt after the encounter, and she comments sardonically that his life has been "full of missed opportunities" (AR 12). As the plot unfolds, we recall this remark and realize, as Mathieu cannot at this stage, that she has already anticipated his reaction to the news of her pregnancy which she is on the point of breaking to him. The question of age will in fact get the lion's share of their conversation that evening, and it is clear that Marcelle has decided that, at her age, she is ready to turn her back on an existence without commitment or responsibility. She proceeds to launch an oblique attack on what she knows to be Mathieu's resistance to any such change. For example, she critically interprets his obsessive tendency to self-analysis as a dishonest attempt to disassociate himself from what he really is masquerading as a superior lucidity—as if lucidity about one's own motives somehow freed one from the burden of assuming responsibility for the consequences of one's choices:

You do it in order to get free from yourself; watching yourself, judging yourself: it's your favorite attitude. When you watch yourself, you reckon that you are not what you are looking at, that you are nothing. In the final analysis, that's your ideal: to be nothing (AR 14).

We recall that to be nothing was also Roquentin's ideal, and there is a real sense in which *Roads to Freedom* is a sustained critique of the anarchistic antisocial character from the earlier novel, although it is also true, as we shall see presently, that some of Roquentin's positions will be retained and vindicated. Mathieu answers defensively that all he wants is to depend on himself alone, to which Marcelle replies, "Yes. To be free. Completely free. That's your vice" (AR 15). But we do not need Marcelle's explicit condemnation of her lover to put Mathieu's position in question. Nor do we need to know the outcome of the *The Age of Reason* to understand the inadequacy of his cheap conception of freedom. Sartre has already made the point at a more subtle, allusive, level: Marcelle occupies a room in her mother's home; every time Mathieu visits Marcelle he comes at night, after Madame Duffy has retired; on this occasion as he creeps up the stairs with his shoes in his hand, he thinks to himself, "What a farce!" (AR 6). Indeed. These two lovers, both in their mid-thirties, have concealed their relationship from Marcelle's mother for seven years. Some freedom! In terms of the opposition between youth and adulthood around which this first volume turns, is there not something flagrantly infantile about this merely furtive defiance of parental authority? Surely his claim to Marcelle, in the course of this night's conversation, that it would seem to him absurd to exist if he did not assume his existence as his very own is preposterous if he is, on the one hand, bold enough (if that is quite the word) to embrace a long-term love affair outside the bounds of bourgeois respectability and yet, on the other hand, too timid to conduct the relationship in broad daylight?

How genuine, how really radical, how carefully thought through, is Mathieu's conception of freedom?

After leaving Marcelle he reflects on the situation in which he now finds himself:

> "A kid. I thought I was giving her pleasure and I've given her a kid. I didn't understand a thing of what I was doing. [The next entire sentence has been inexplicably omitted in Eric Sutton's translation.] Now I'm going to give four hundred francs to this old woman, she is going to plunge her instrument between Marcelle's legs and scrape; life will depart as it came; and I, I will be a stupid prick as before; in destroying this life, no more than in creating it, I will not have known what I was doing." He let out a short, dry laugh, "And other guys? Those who have decided in all seriousness to be fathers and who feel themselves to be progenitors when they look at their wife's belly, do they understand any better than I? They went at it blindly, with three flicks of their dicks. The rest is work in a darkroom and in gelatin, like photography. They have no part in it" (AR 23–24).

This evinces the same loathing for natural processes which we have already encountered in *Nausea:* there is the same scandalized reaction to any form of existence that is not entirely informed by human intention. That an embryo might develop quite independently of human volition is a fact which places an intolerable limit on freedom. But, Sartre is implying, this is a singularly *inhuman* conception of freedom, for God alone—if such an entity exists, and for Sartre it emphatically does not—God alone is that entity which can claim to be *causa sui,* its own cause. The drunk who had wanted to enlist in the fight against the fascist forces of Franco in the Spanish Civil War and who had not managed to do so—for reasons unknown to us—but let us suppose even that the reason were pusillanimity—has been introduced by Sartre as standing for a more authentic and attractive implicit conception of freedom to the extent that the man has resorted to drink because he has recognized either his impotence or his ignominy (we do not know which and it does not matter) and therefore wishes to obliterate his unbearable humanity (for Sartre, his moral responsibility) by sinking into a subhuman brutish stupor. The subject of drunkenness will be raised elsewhere in the trilogy on more than one occasion. Halfway through *The Age of Reason* Mathieu explains to Ivich's brother—who admires his alcoholic capacity—that he doesn't get drunk because "I don't know how to let myself go, I always have to think about everything which happens to me, it's a defense" (AR 220), an admission which effectively endorses Marcelle's criticisms of him at the outset of the book. Reflecting on the matter, he realizes that he clings to his "human dignity. . . . He was afraid that if he let himself go he might suddenly find in his head . . . a fly's thought" (AR 219).

B. Existentialist Gender Ideology Revised: Towards a Feminine Individual and History[4]

In sharp contrast to Mathieu's attitude to nature and life as a natural process, Marcelle has a more positive response. Retching into a basin one day with morning sickness, she watches the vomit slowly running toward the drain hole and thinks, "'Weird!' It didn't disgust her: it was *life,* like the sticky efflorescences of spring, it wasn't any more repulsive than the little sticky reddish and redolent gum which covered the buds" (AR 86). We have already seen that the opposition between youth and adulthood and that between a simplistic and irresponsible conception of freedom and one which is responsibly engaged are intertwined. These organizational oppositions are now further enriched and overlaid by a third opposition, between masculine and feminine conceptions of natural life and freedom.

In order to investigate this new opposition it will be necessary to recall a couple of features of what one might call our cultural unconscious—that is, those decisive components of our ways of ordering and interpreting the world which are so constitutive of our views of things as to remain inaccessible to awareness under most circumstances. It will be recalled that after leaving Marcelle's room on the first night of the book, Mathieu reflects that the worst of it is that whether he creates life by making Marcelle pregnant or whether he destroys it in the course of arranging an abortion he will have been the "dupe of circumstances" (*couillon*) to the extent that he will not have known what he was doing. The French expression is actually considerably more forceful and choice than the rather pallid translation offered here (*couillon* originally meant "testicle," and *couille* still does), and the nearest American English equivalent, in a similar scatological register, would be a composite of "stupid prick," "jerk," and "I will be fucked in the ass." Both the French and English popular expressions mobilize a fundamental assumption about human sexuality, gender identity, and the nature of human activity which has been dominant (although by no means monolithically so) for centuries in many if not most post-Neo-

lithic cultures and are only now being widely challenged: namely, that forceful, successful, rational activity is predominantly the domain of men rather than
women. This is especially obvious in the third English
expression, as passive homosexuality has always been
considered in traditional homophobia to be a form of
feminization and thereby an egregious abdication from
male prerogative. This is no less true of the French
expression, which mobilizes and perpetuates an entire
gender ideology by means of a process Freud frequently had occasion to draw attention to in the course
of his investigations of dreams.[5] To call someone a testicle, and mean thereby that one is a fool or a dupe, is
to suggest that one is—if we may bend a colloquialism
to our needs here—"not quite all there" in a crudely
scatalogical sense of the expression: one has lost all of
his faculties and physical attributes except one testicle
(or, one's brains have descended to his testicle, or one
has no more intelligence than a testicle, all of which
amount to the same thing). Given the patent impossibility of the latter, what is really meant by the expression is that someone has been separated from the testicle in question (how else can a testicle exist on its
own?)—in other words, castrated. Freud's investigations of infantile sexuality—the Oedipus complex, penis envy in little girls, and so on[6]—suggested that, in
a society where males are more highly esteemed and
enjoy greater privileges than women, children develop
a phantasy about the female genitalia to the effect that
women are really just castrated males. The French expression *couillon* reiterates this view by suggesting
that to be an inadequate agent (someone's or something's dupe) is to be a mutilated male or (and this

amounts to the same thing in the gender ideology underpinning the expression) a woman.

We have already seen, in the chapter on *Nausea,* the extent to which Sartre—like the rest of us—was the more or less unwitting accomplice of mainstream sexism. One of the important and interesting things about the trilogy is the extent to which Sartre has undertaken an implicit critique of his earlier position on this subject. Insofar as the trilogy, as its title suggests, unfolds before us the progressive apprenticeship of freedom by the main characters, it is interesting to observe that Mathieu's apprenticeship of what for Sartre is *real* freedom, and not the trite travesty of it which Mathieu subscribes to in the first volume, entails learning a more "feminine" conception of freedom. This becomes especially clear when we examine the most extended and powerful evocation of freedom in the trilogy. Significantly, this is made by a woman, Odette, Mathieu's sister-in-law. After years of living under the domination of her thoroughly odious husband, Jacques, deferring to him in all things, and, most especially, relying on him to decide for her what the meaning of the world—*her* world—was, she is unexpectedly liberated by the sudden realization that his domineering know-it-all ways are a bluff and that he is really a pitiful coward. In the exodus from Paris in the face of the advancing German army the couple have lost their way; they decide to stop their car at the edge of a forest in order to try and get some sleep:

> He turned round, crossed his arms on the steering wheel and let his head drop on his hands. She remained seated, upright, oppressed: she was waiting

and watching. . . . She could not think of anything for as long as he remained awake with that image of her in his head; I have never been able to think of anything when he was near me. There we are: he had let out *his* three grunts; she relaxed a little. . . . He was asleep, the war was asleep, the world of men was asleep swallowed up in that head; upright in the shadow, between the chalky light coming from the two windows, deep in a pool of moonlight, Odette kept her vigil. A very old memory came to mind: I was running on a little pink path, I was twelve years old, I stopped, my heart beating with an anxious joy, and I said out aloud, "I am indispensable." She repeated, "I am indispensable," but she didn't know to what; she tried to think of the war, it seemed to her that she was going to discover the truth: "Is it true [as Jacques had declared to her] that our victory would simply serve the interests of the Russians?" She gave up the effort at once and her joy turned into disgust: "I don't know enough to decide."

She wanted to smoke. She didn't really want to, it was nervousness. The urge grew and grew, taking her by the throat. An overwhelming and peremptory urge like those of her imperious childhood; he has put the packet in his coat pocket. Why should he smoke? That taste of tobacco, in his mouth, must be so boring, so conventional, why should he smoke rather than I? She leaned over him; he was breathing heavily, she slid her hand in his pocket, took out the cigarettes, then gently opened the door pushing back the catch and slid out. The moon seen through the leaves, the pools of moonlight on the road, this cool air, that cry of an animal, it's all *mine*. She lit a cigarette. The war is asleep, Berlin is asleep, Moscow, Churchill, the Politbureau, our political leaders are asleep, everything is asleep, nobody sees *my* night, I am indispensable. . . . She suddenly realized that she detested tobacco; she took two more puffs and then threw the cigarette away: she no longer even knew why she had wanted to smoke. The foliage rustled softly, the countryside creaked like a wooden floor. The stars were like animals: she was afraid; he was asleep and she had rediscovered the dark world of her childhood, the forest of questions without answers; it was he who knew the names of the stars, the exact distance of the moon from the earth, the number of inhabitants in the region, their history and their occupations; he is asleep, I despise him and I know nothing; she felt herself lost in a world of which she could make no use, in that world which existed to be *seen* and *touched*. She ran back to the car, she wanted to wake him immediately, she wanted to awaken Science, Industry and Morality. She put her hand on the door-handle, she leaned against the door and saw, through the window, a big open mouth. "What's the use?" she said to herself (TS 215–216).

Odette realizes here that whatever the complexity of the historical meaning of the war and her lack of understanding of the gigantic events shaking Europe, whatever the relative insignificance of her role in the war, she, and she alone, will always in the final analysis be responsible for deciding *what it means to her*. "I am indispensable." Because Jacques, through whose eyes she has always docilely interpreted and understood everything of "a man's world"—politics, warfare, "Science, Industry"—is asleep, and because she now despises him anyway, she is free —in this rare moment of solitude, jolted out of her routine existence by the exodus, in the face of a mysterious and faintly threatening nocturnal landscape which is outside of her usual experience—to confront the fact that for any of this to have any meaning at all, *she* must choose those meanings. Not unnaturally she finds the experience both exhilarating and anxiety provoking; and, indeed, the passage constitutes an excellent example of what Heidegger called angst, or "dread": those rare moments when—instead of trundling through our lives relying on habit, routine, or the conventional values and goals with which the society in which we live constantly solicits us to get through them—we come face to face with the realization that we alone are responsible for our lives. And that this is true no matter how deeply imbricated we may be within, and informed through and through by, the culture to which we belong, the contemporary historical moment or our childhood experiences. "Nobody sees *my* night, I am indispensable."

Interestingly Odette, in the middle of all this, is briefly tempted—in the face of the sudden disgust she feels at her inability to answer any of the questions the night poses to her—to flee freedom's perpetually open-ended, provisional (and thereby disquietening) condition by turning for solace to a cigarette as an appropriately phallic synecdoche of her husband and his reassuring but futile knowledge, which she pulls out of his clothing. She immediately recognizes the inadequacy of this palliative, however, discards it, and returns to confront "the forest of the questions without answers." (Significantly, while this symbolic castration of Jacques and the incipient, or nascent, empowerment of Odette mobilizes the standard panoply of symbols denoting that castration anxiety, as analyzed by Freud, which has been one of the foundations of a phallogocentric cultural order—Jacques's penis/cigarette is removed, thrown away, and when Odette returns to the car all she sees is the gaping wound of his open mouth where the cigarette might normally be—there seems to be a willingness on Sartre's part to go beyond the phallic Law altogether: rather than usurp the reassuring omniscient place of the Father as phallic mother, Odette accedes to genuine freedom by discarding the patriarchal law of the phallus altogether.) As the contrasted counterpart to Jacques's trivial knowledge, the metaphorical forest, as well as the literal nocturnal forest scene here,[7] serves the same functions as Marcelle's pregnancy, the vomit of her morning sickness, and the mysterious life of the embryo which scandalizes Mathieu. These phenomena all confront male desire as it is represented in the book—the desire, that is, to dominate and subordinate all life and all existence such that the latter reflect in every last detail the pattern of an imperial project which is always transparent to itself without any residue of the merely contingent or *given*—in short, the desire to be God—with its fundamental impossibility and folly. (This critique of the male project is also brought to bear on Brunet in the second half of *Troubled Sleep:* for example, in the failure of his attempt to subordinate his body to the ascetic and masochistic discipline he inflicts upon it in the prison camp, and in the hostile reaction he arouses from the other men to his anxious puritanical aversion to expressions of sexual desire and his authoritarianism in general.)

Mathieu's evolution toward an understanding of this is initiated by his attempts to come to terms with the imminent war for which he is mobilized in *The Reprieve*. In the following crucial passage he is standing, smoking a cigar, in the corridor of a coach of the night train which is taking him up to Paris to join his regiment:

Everything which had got to him up to that point had been man-size, the minor pains-in-the-ass and the catastrophes, he had seen them coming, he had met them face to face. When he had gone to take the money in Lola's room, he had seen the banknotes, he had touched them, he had breathed the perfume which floated in the room; and when he had dumped Marcelle, he had looked her in the eye while he spoke to her; his difficulties had only ever been with himself; he had been able to say to himself, "I was right, I was wrong"; he could judge himself. Now that had become impossible.... He thought, "I am setting off for the war" and that didn't mean anything. Something had happened which was too much for him to understand. The war was too much for him to understand. "It's not so much that it is too much for me to understand as it's that the war is not here. Where is it? Everywhere: it is being born everywhere, the train is driving itself into the war, these vacationers in their white linen are walking in the war, there is not a single heartbeat which does not feed it, not a single human consciousness which is not traversed by it.... From time to time one thinks that one is going to touch it, on any old thing.... One puts out one's hand, it is no longer there.... Ah! he thought to himself, one would have to be everywhere at once.... Gloomily he surveyed the end of his cigar: everywhere, without which one is duped, one does not know what is going on.... One

would have have to be everywhere, I would have to
see myself from everywhere, from Berlin as one
three millionth of the French army, through
Gomez's eyes as one of those French bastards who
have to be driven into battle by means of kicks,
through the eyes of Odette. I would have to see myself through the eyes of the war. But where are the
eyes of the war? I am here, before my eyes large
illuminated surfaces slide.... I see—and yet I am
groping blindly and every one of my movements
lights up bulbs and sets off bells in a world which I
cannot see.... An enormous entity, a planet, in a
space with one hundred million dimensions; three-
dimensional beings couldn't even imagine it. And
yet each dimension was an autonomous center of
awareness. If one were to try to look at the planet
directly, it would disintegrate into fragments, only
centers of awareness would remain. A hundred million free centers of awareness of which each one was
busy contemplating walls, the glowing tip of a cigar,
familiar faces, and was busy constructing its destiny
on its own responsibility. And yet, if one were one
of these centers of awareness one realized, thanks
to imperceptible contacts and insensible changes,
that one was the accomplice of a gigantic and invisible polyp. The war: each person is free and yet the
die is cast. It is here, it is everywhere, it is the totality of all my thoughts, and all the words of Hitler,
all the actions of Gomez: but nobody is here to add
it all up. It exists only for God. But God doesn't exist.
And yet the war exists (R 322–26).

It is this realization—that his personal destiny does
not depend solely on one-on-one interpersonal interac-
tions and the kinds of decisions these entail (should
he or should he not steal the money from Lola, for

example), but that his fate is merely one infinitesimal dimension of a gigantic process which is almost that of a unified organism (a "polyp")—so true is it that every individual activity is relentlessly integrated into it and endowed with a meaning which comes to it from the war as a total signifying context—it is this realization which first challenges the individualistic conception of freedom which Mathieu subscribes to at the outset of the novel and its accompanying desire to be God which he explicitly points to here as the only existential condition which could ever, albeit impossibly, fulfill his desires. The parallel with Mathieu's reaction to Marcelle's pregnancy (to participate in such biological processes is to be the dupe of circumstances because the growth of an embryo is something that does not depend on the will of a human agent) is made quite deliberately in the passage just quoted from *The Reprieve* when Mathieu reflects that unless one can be omnipresent, one will once again not understand what is happening or be the master of one's destiny.

It should be mentioned that in the passage just quoted Sartre anticipates the positions of the next generation of philosophers to dominate intellectual life in France after Sartre fell from grace in the French public's eyes somewhere around 1960. Writers like Jacques Derrida and Luce Irigaray have worked on the secret textual complicities which unite a certain philosophical conception of truth, or reality—that the truth, or reality, is the presence of the object in front of a knowing subject (for example, Mathieu's cigar he is smoking, or Marcelle standing in front of him)—and a certain gender ideology which Freud perfectly articulated (without really questioning it). Thus, the anxiety

which, according to Freud, male children felt upon seeing the female genitals (a horrifying absence of the
penis, implying castration) and the envy which female
children felt upon seeing the male genitals became, as
a consequence of the work of the critics of "phallogo-
centrism," merely some of the means, culturally induced, whereby men eventually acceded to their social
roles as masters of knowledge (defined primitively as
the presence or absence of the thing in front of one [a
more highly developed version would be Aristotle's
Law of Identity—A cannot be both A and - A]) and
women were assigned their roles as bearers of children, which unconsciously symbolize an acquisition of
the penis or consolation for its lack. To the extent that,
in the scene under discussion, Mathieu morosely contemplates his cigar as the very symbol of the inadequacy of a phallogocentric conception of knowledge
Sartre anticipates the work of his successors. The latter have advanced, however, as an alternative to phal-
lomorphic knowledge, a conception of all entities (both
the subject and object of a more traditional philosophy)
which is that of endlessly deferred *relation* (most often
designated in contemporary thought by the term
différance). The fundamental change this entails can
be graphically and powerfully illustrated (as has been
done by Irigaray, for example)[8] if one adopts the va-
gina as one's implicit metaphor for knowledge rather
than the penis. The former is constituted by two lips
in such a way as to invalidate an Aristotelian logic of
identity because the "entity" in question, from a phal-
locentric point of view, is distressingly insubstantial
and incomprehensible: unlike a penis, it cannot be

grasped as a solid real thing (indeed, according to masculine logic, as a hole it appears to be nothing or no
thing), and to the extent that it is anything at all it is
constituted as such by relations between other things
(lips, walls, etc.) which are nonetheless indisputably
part of what it is. To the extent that what Sartre offers
us as an alternative (albeit an impossible one) to the
invalidated cigar—the sum total of all the millions of
points of view which he believes constitutes the reality, or truth, of the war (partially achieved for the
reader of *The Reprieve*)—to the extent that this alternative is still presented in terms of the knowledge of
perceiving subjects (rather than in terms of the infinitely deferred relations between all the entities involved in the war which make those entities what they
are, including the human subjects)—to this extent Sartre is still working within a phallogocentric mode.

By the second half of *The Reprieve*, Mathieu is already halfway toward accepting the limits of his condition; that to be *couillonné*—that is, to be "feminine"
or the dupe and victim of circumstances beyond one's
control—is fundamental to the human condition, without, however, this fact being a facile justification for
quietism and passivity. In *Troubled Sleep* we find
Mathieu finally confronting what for Sartre is this
more realistic, and more humane, assessment of the
nature of freedom. He has just engaged in an argument
with one of his fellow soldiers on the subject of their
personal responsibility for the defeat of France. He
concludes that each one of them has had the war they
deserve and that, in his own case, his fault has been
the attitude he had already expressed at the end of the

107

first chapter of *The Age of Reason:* never really committing himself wholeheartedly to the life which was in fact his, always saving himself, holding himself back, for some special occasion which never materialized:

> His sole aim had been to keep himself available. For an act. A free and self-conscious act which would engage his whole life and which would be the beginning of a new existence. He had never been able to get completely involved in a love affair, a pleasure.... He was waiting. And meanwhile, slowly, furtively, the years had crept up on him and taken him from behind.... "I should have committed myself at twenty-five. Like Brunet. Yes, but in those circumstances one does not commit oneself having watertight reasons and knowing completely what one is getting into. One becomes the dupe and victim of circumstances." ... He had thought of leaving for Russia, dropping his studies, learning a manual trade. But what had held him back each time, on the verge of these violent ruptures, was the fact that he lacked *reasons* for doing it.... And he had continued to wait (AR 64).

Now, his ability to assess the consequences of this failure to engage himself wonderfully concentrated by the sentence which the defeat of France has passed on him individually, he appreciates for the first time the necessary and inevitable limitations and constraints under which authentic action always operates:

> How I would like to plunge into an unknown act as if into a forest. An act. An act which would engage one and which one never understands entirely (TS 97)

Mathieu has accepted that his desire always to "see straight" (TS 96)—to be in full possession of all the data which could conceivably be relevant to the making of any decision (especially a lucid understanding of his own motives)—is not only impossible but, as we shall see more clearly later, ultimately crippling and an excuse for inaction. More forcefully than in the long passage from *The Reprieve,* Mathieu accepts "feminization" to the extent that in mainstream sexist discourse one of the dimensions of being feminine consists in not being in control of one's destiny. Mathieu's acceptance of a more feminine conception of freedom is made clear at two levels: first, the "unknown act" into which one might plunge "as into a forest" intentionally recalls Odette's great discovery of freedom at the edge of a forest analyzed above; second, forests are regularly associated with the female genitals in our culture. Freud pointed this out,[9] but we do not need to turn to an authority outside the Sartrean corpus to establish this; we have already seen, in the chapter on *Nausea,* the extent to which for Sartre trees and gardens were associated with feminine sexuality or, at best, failed virility.[10] The difference here is that the association no longer provokes disgust but, on the contrary, is presented in a description which suggests both the embrace of the feminine by a male in an act of love and a synthesis of male and female on terms of equality in a novel vision of viable human activity. Finally, the wish expressed here will in fact be realized in the unfinished fourth volume when Mathieu and Odette become lovers and achieve an emotional fulfillment neither had known before.[11]

C. Death, Authenticity, and Freedom

A qualification should perhaps be added at this point. Nothing in the passage we have just examined, nor its meaning in terms of the book as a whole which we have just examined, and Mathieu's subsequent decision to join Pinette in a suicidal last stand which this passage is leading up to, constitutes an endorsement of irrationalism. (Nor does the passage endorse the "terroristic" freedom of his last stand; such freedom as he mobilizes in that situation is pointless and, as all that he has left, is a direct consequence of the futility of the life he has chosen up to this point.) Simply at this point in time, and in these circumstances, the objective situation in which Mathieu finds himself—a useless member of a useless military unit—does not present him with any rational or practical solution to his fundamental problem: the futility of his existence (for which he alone has been responsible). The deliberate assumption of this condition in a suicidal gesture—choosing to die unnecessarily in order to underline the nullity of his life—is the only minimal form of mastery of his condition left to him (rather than passive resignation). As in *Nausea,* however, the final frank confrontation with meaninglessness—especially the ultimate absurd enigma, death itself—constitutes a liberation from bad faith and inauthenticity, a kind of wiping the slate clean which enables one to start afresh as an authentic agent for the first time. Sartre's didactic intention in keeping Mathieu alive after his last stand is clear: as Orestes puts it in the *The Flies,* "Human life begins on the far side of despair" (F, 123). It is his having passed through the tempering fire of death which makes his rebirth—the engagement in the Resistance, the relationship with Odette, and all the rest—possible.

This idea that only once one has *really* accepted the fact that one is going to die—at a visceral level rather than as a purely intellectual proposition; that only once one has faced death resolutely as one's "ownmost possibility," as Heidegger put it, does one accede to genuine freedom and a kind of grim salvation—this notion is common to all the great "existentialist" writers: Camus, Sartre, de Beauvoir, Malraux, and others. In the trilogy it is a central preoccupation, and Mathieu is not alone in being subjected to this ultimate test. Lola, the nightclub singer and lover of Mathieu's young acolyte, Boris, is only able to find the resolution to face an inevitable separation from her much younger lover—and in fact will choose to give him his freedom when he has offered to marry her— because she has just discovered that she has a tumor in her womb. The victory is all the more remarkable to the extent that she is alone in the world, survives by virtue of her voice and her fast-fading looks in a precarious world of tenuous nightclub engagements, and regularly takes refuge in heroin. Lola is clearly destined to be one of life's victims. The twenty-year-old Boris, who is half her age, represents everything that she has lost and that threatens her: namely, the careless, thoughtlessly cruel, narcissistic and egocentric indifference which is natural to youth because it believes itself immortal and invulnerable. For this very reason she *must* have him. As a symbolic repossession of youth. And, of course, for this reason she is doomed to pursue a mirage: their relationship is characterized

111

by her insatiable pursuit of something Boris cannot give her:

> "Boris, you are all I have, I'm alone in the world, you must love me.... When I think of my life I want to drown myself, I have to think of you all day long. Don't be mean to me." ... Boris ... perceived the situation clearly. "If you are alone, it is because it's what you want, it's because you are proud. If it weren't for that you would love a guy older than yourself. Me, I'm too young, I can't prevent you from being alone. I suspect that you even chose me for that very reason" (AR 45–46).

Just as it was in order to flee the acknowledgment of the possibility of death which hovers permanently on the horizon of all our lives that Lola had fallen in love with Boris in the first place, so her readiness to confront death eventually releases her from his spell. As she puts it, "He talks to me, he screws me, but I'll die alone" (TS 233).

Boris himself is busy evading freedom and the recognition of death with an assiduity similar to that of the other characters. His case is deceptive, however, because he appears to have acknowledged the reality of death. Indeed, he is convinced that he will die in his early twenties. Seated in a bar one night during the Munich crisis of September 1938, he engages in the following reflections:

> Boris counted on his fingers: "26, 27, 28, 29, 30, I will come back here five more times and that will be it; I will never see the Basque Bar again." It was weird. Five times. He would drink white rums five more times at this table and then it would be the war, the

Basque Bar would be closed and, in October 39, Boris would mobilized.... At the moment of his death, in 42, he would have lunched 365 x 22 times, that is to say 8,030 times, counting his meals as a suckling infant. And if one assumed that he had eaten omelettes one time out of every 10 meals, he would have eaten 803 omelettes. "Only 803 omelettes?" he said to himself with astonishment. Ah no! there would also be the dinners, so that would make 16,060 meals and 1,606 omelettes.... He had always known that he would die young. He had often told himself that he would end up with tuberculosis or murdered by Lola. But, in his heart of hearts, he had never doubted that he would be killed in war (R 271–72).

How, in these circumstances, can we speak of an *unwillingness* to face death? In fact, this ostensibly obsessional concern with confronting imminent death is really a palliative designed to deaden the secret anxiety which underlies it: how reassuring death would be if its moment of accomplishment were in fact foreseeable in this manner, merely the realization of an inner certitude on the part of the individual in question! Rather than the inherently unforeseeable event which, by definition, never arrives at a convenient time but, on the contrary, is always shockingly surprising, strictly independent of our wills (except in the case of suicide), very inconvenient, and, if one is an atheist, scandalously *absurd,* meaningless, as incomprehensible as life itself. A frank visceral recognition of this stubborn fact makes counting how many omelettes one will have eaten by the time one dies ludicrous. Which is why Boris's engaging in these kinds of computation is a sure sign that he is evading such a recognition. If further proof of this were required, we need only recall his disarray when he discovers what he thinks is Lola's corpse (she is in fact in a drug-induced coma): he is devastated not by the loss of his lover but by death itself.

D. Youth versus Adulthood

As we have seen in the case of Mathieu, the opposition between youth and adulthood is one of the major organizational techniques in terms of which Sartre illustrates his characters' slow apprenticeship of (or deficiencies with respect to) genuine freedom. Boris's relations with both Lola and Mathieu consistently betray traces of an infantile dependence on adults. For example, in an early chapter of *The Age of Reason* we see him reflecting on his relationship with Lola:

> "She's funny," thought Boris, "She is ashamed of loving me because she is older than me. I, on the other hand, I find that natural, one party has to be older than the other." Above all, it was more moral: Boris would not have known how to love a woman his own age. "If both are young, they don't know how to behave, they blunder along, one always has the impression of playing house. With older people, it's not the same. They are dependable, they guide you and then their love has weight" (AR 32).

Or again, after Mathieu and Brunet (the former's communist journalist friend) exclude him from a conversation they want to have in private, Boris is briefly tempted, in an access of jealousy, to put his relationship with Mathieu, whom he adores and emulates, in question: he speculates as to whether Mathieu might

114

not conceivably have been mistaken about life in general and has now decided to convert to communism. Significantly, he dismisses these speculations as futile: "Mathieu wasn't the sort to be in the wrong" (AR 179). Part of the reasoning which enables him to dismiss as improbable Mathieu's conversion to communism is that the latter had already discouraged a brief high school flirtation with communism on Boris's part:

> Mathieu had turned him away from it by explaining what freedom was. Boris had understood at once: one had the duty to do all one wants to do, to think whatever one likes, to be responsible only to oneself and to put in question, constantly, everything one thinks and everybody. Boris had constructed his life on this and he was scrupulously free: in particular, he always put everyone in question, except Mathieu and Ivich; those two it was pointless to put in question given that they were perfect (AR 179).

As in the case of his preoccupation with death, Boris's belief in the importance of freedom is really an evasion: a *belief*—that is, an absence of real thought, of freedom—which does not really entail putting anything into question; a mere submission to someone else's intellectual authority.

While Boris is happy to disburden himself of the anxieties and uncertainties attendant upon genuine freedom by letting adults decide for him the answers to the big questions which existence throws at us, he nonetheless resists fiercely any understanding of what it is like to be one of those adults in question. Faced with a moment of unhappiness on the part of Lola, he strenuously resists facing what is really implied by adult suffering: "It must be a question of age.... Old folks are embittered, you would think that it is always their lives which are at stake" (AR 36). This is, of course, the one thing about his own life which Boris won't face: that it is indeed always "at stake." The passage continues:

> Once, when Boris was small, he had dropped his spoon; he had been told to pick it up and he had refused, he had been stubborn. At which point his father had said, in a tone of unforgettable majesty, "Well then, *I* will pick it up." Boris had seen a large body bending with difficulty, the bald top of a head, he had heard cracking joints, it was an intolerable sacrilege: he had burst into tears. Ever since, Boris had considered adults as voluminous and impotent divinities.... If they slipped and fell one was torn between the desire to laugh and religious horror. And if they had tears in their eyes, like Lola at this moment, one didn't know where to put oneself (AR 36).

That adults might conceivably be vulnerable, mortal, fallible, that above all they might be prey to the same confusions and sufferings as children, and that just like children they never stop learning and never really feel that they have all the answers (that they "have grown up")—this is deeply threatening to any child who depends upon the security of parental authority to get through life. This is the primary reason why Boris is so anxious about aging: he does not want to be forced to discover—when he can no longer plausibly go on being the acolyte of someone like Mathieu—that, as Odette puts it, he is indispensable, that he alone must decide what the answers are and that such answers as he provides must of necessity remain provisional, that there are no easy certitudes, that reality is always ambiguous, always a problem, open-ended, messy, imperfect, and mostly mediocre, without any of the aesthetic perfection of the straightforward neatly arranged little life he has imagined for himself with its conveniently easy death at age twenty-two. The belief in an early death ensures that the problem which is adulthood will never arise. This is also why he experiences his keenest sense of freedom when he is busy shoplifting: in much the same way as Mathieu—in his purely furtive transgression of settled married existence—seems to need to engage in a defiance of the social order which recognizes the ultimate authority of the latter in the very moment when he defies it (instead of setting his own terms for the relationship with Marcelle in the course of an open challenge to the established order), Boris is confirmed in his ultimately infantile irresponsibility by this gratuitous act of transgression which recognizes and reaffirms the social order of private property by its strictly clandestine character. Even the hint of incestuous desire in his relations with his sister, Ivich, implies a preference for remaining within the charmed circle of the family of his childhood over and against assuming that necessity of breaking out of it which has been traditionally associated with adulthood in most societies.

Like those of everyone else, however, Boris's chickens finally come home to roost, and he too has to face reality. He does indeed, as he had anticipated, go off to war; he even gets wounded; however, he inconveniently *survives*. Here we see him lying in his hospital bed, morosely trying to come to terms with his survival:

> As far as he was concerned, he had died at Sedan in May 1940: the trouble was all these years which remained to him to live. He sighed again, watched a big green fly which was walking across the ceiling, and concluded, "I'm a mediocrity." This idea was profoundly distasteful. Up to that point Boris had made a point of never putting himself in question and it had suited his purposes admirably; on the other hand, for as long as it had been merely a question of getting himself decently and neatly killed, his being a mediocrity had not been of much importance. On the contrary, there was less to regret. But now everything had changed: he was destined to live and he was obliged to recognize that he was without vocation, money or talent.... The fly made off, buzzing loudly, and Boris passed his hand under his shirt and stroked the scar which crossed his stomach close to his groin; he liked to feel the small ravine of flesh under his fingers (TS 61–62).

The faintly masturbatory overtones of his fondly stroking the scar near his crotch clearly suggest the function his preoccupation with death had served.

Ivich's strategy for living resembles that of her brother. While he flees life by imagining a premature death for himself, she avoids the necessity of creating and choosing her own future—with its inevitable attendant risk of failure—by embracing failure *now:*

> "I can't imagine my future. It's blocked." ... Mathieu watched her in silence.... It was true that she had no future: Ivich at thirty, Ivich at forty, that made no sense.... When Mathieu was alone or when

> he talked to Daniel or Marcelle, his life stretched
> before him, obvious and monotonous: a few women,
> a few voyages, some books.... When he saw Ivich,
> he seemed to live a catastrophe. Ivich was a small
> voluptuous and tragic suffering without a tomorrow
> (AR 70–71).

Thus, she fails her exams, becomes pregnant by a man
she despises, and marries into his no less detestable
family. This is certainly perverse, and perhaps difficult
to understand; but as a strategy for living it has its
advantages: to try and make a success of one's life requires courage in the face of adversity, perseverance,
and patience. Most difficult of all, it entails that when
the chips are down and the outcome has finally been
decided, and one has to judge whether on the whole
one's life has been worth living, in most instances one
is going to have to attribute at least some measure of
the success or failure of the global enterprise to oneself. These are the normal conditions of the mobilization of one's existential freedom, and they are precisely
what Ivich is able to flee by allowing herself to drift
from one disaster to another:

> Ivich hated leaving places and people, even when she
> loathed them, because she was afraid of the future.
> She would abandon herself with a sullen indolence
> to the most unpleasant situations and she would end
> up by finding a kind of respite in them (AR 94).

Never having undertaken anything, she hopes she will
never have to blame herself for the failure of her life.
This is rightly presented to us as a flight from life
itself:

> Mathieu looked as his watch. "Ten forty, she's late."
> He didn't like her being late, he was always afraid
> that she might have inadvertently died. She always
> forgot everything, she was constantly fleeing from
> herself.... She forgot to eat, she forgot to sleep. One
> day she would forget to breath and that would be
> that (AR 65).

Here we have the explanation of so much else of Ivich's
behavior: her unusually intense dislike of having to
support the gaze of other people (which manifests itself
by her constantly veiling her face with her hair); her
frequent resentment of people's mere presence (she declares, for example, that expositions of famous paint-
ings should not be opened to the public for this reason);
her eye irritation in the presence of sunlight which is
a psychosomatic reaction to that which makes her visible to others and which thereby makes interaction
with them possible; her dislike of physical contact with
people; her sexual frigidity (she is rarely attracted to
men and does not act on the fact that she is occasionally attracted to women, although she takes care to
mention her homosexual desires in the presence of
men who desire her); her sadism (witness the last-men-
tioned habit). Her sadism constitutes a response to the
anxiety provoked by being an object of the gaze of others by that attempt to transform others in their turn
into objects of which sadism is merely the most extreme form and to which it is the logical conclusion.

It should be mentioned here that the symptoms just
described are regularly encountered as components in
the makeup of individuals who have been oppressed,
by people who feel that the embracing of failure is the
only form of freedom available to them. Thus, for ex-

ample, as is described in greater detail below, none of the women in the trilogy seem to be endowed with real futures (essentially a male prerogative—the extension in time of an active project), and Ivich resembles oppressed characters like the lesbian Inès in *No Exit* and the homosexual Daniel of the trilogy in embracing failure and sadism. Ivich's oppression as a woman is only vaguely alluded to, when, toward the end of *The Reprieve,* it becomes clear that her panic in the face of the impending war (which is generated by her complete incomprehension of it as a geopolitical phenomenon) is the product of a sexist education and gender role: she has not the faintest idea where Czechoslovakia is on the map of Europe, and, in a move which anticipates the similar (but more powerful) realization on the part of Jessica Barine in *Dirty Hands* of her gendered identity, she has a glimpse of the truth and gives vent to her exasperation ("I don't know a thing about it, I've been kept in the dark, they made me learn Latin and no one has told me anything" (R 360).

It is perhaps difficult to understand why Mathieu— or indeed anyone else—should be attracted to this young woman. The attraction is easily understood, however, once one recalls Mathieu's global situation and project at this point in his life: what he wants above all is to cling to his vanished youth and flee anything remotely resembling responsibility. Under these circumstances Ivich is fatally attractive to him: he knows that he is increasingly an ordinary almost middle-aged man, predictable, set in his ways, a civil servant with a secure job and the prospect of a secure pension. Marriage to Marcelle and paternity will be the last nail in the coffin of his youth. Precisely because Ivich is incapable of loving anyone, let alone himself, and because she is impossible, irresponsible, willfully and wantonly wasteful of her young life in the way that youth alone is capable of (see, for example, the scene in the Sumatra club where she plunges a knife into her hand—an act which Mathieu, at his wits' end in the face of the impasse his life has come to represent, feels compelled to imitate), she incarnates or symbolizes Mathieu's impossible salvation from his mediocre, middle-aged, middle-class destiny: if he can persuade her to be fascinated by him, then he will miraculously recover the freedom of his own youth and his own irresponsibility.

E. Alienation to the Internalized Gaze of the Other: Daniel and Sadomasochism

Ivich's sadism is as haphazard as her young life is in general. That of Daniel Sereno, however, has the staying power and persistence of a choice which constitutes a permanent and desperate search for a solution to an intolerable existential torment: Daniel is a homosexual in an age and a society where homosexuality is necessarily almost always clandestine outside of rare and tiny coteries or marginal groupings. Which means that he has inevitably internalized the loathing of homosexuality of the homophobic society in which he lives. To be a product of this society, and homosexual, is unwittingly to install one's tormentors in one's own mind. As Daniel himself puts it, when he finally confesses his homosexuality to Mathieu:

I am ashamed of being a homosexual *because I am* a homosexual. I know what you're going to say: "If I were in your place, I wouldn't stand for any non-sense. I would claim my place in the sun, it's a personal taste like any other," and so on and so forth. But that is all entirely off the mark. You say that kind of thing precisely because you are not a homosexual. All homosexuals are ashamed of being so, it's part of their makeup (AR 393).

To attribute this socially induced shame to his innate or inherent nature is of course erroneous (an error which is a significant component of Daniel's flight from freedom, as we shall see presently); but as far as Daniel and the other victims of this kind of social conditioning are concerned, it comes to much the same thing: namely, that his most imperious desires and most intense pleasures will always—not just on reflection, but most especially when they take him by the throat—appear to him as despicable and loathsome, however much he may rage against an unjust sentence which he is paradoxically carrying out upon himself at the behest of others. The result is a personality which is in a permanent state of civil war: he is at one and the same time his own sadistic torturer and masochistic victim. In order to put a definitive end to this intolerable situation there is in fact only one real solution: to recognize that in order to have internalized public opinion he must have been its accomplice. Even if, of course, he unwittingly (and quite naturally and excusably) adopted the prejudices and conventional values of the world in which he grew up, *he and he alone* chose to internalize them, to grant them that silent and apparently innocuous and effortless acquiescence which constitutes acceptance and internalization. Even if to have been in a position to reject them

123

or question them as a child would have required that other values be available to him as alternatives, or that he exist in a problematic relation to the figures of authority or objects of his love such that he be driven to put them in question and forge new values of his own, even if all this would have been necessary for him to subscribe to different values and if none of this was in fact available to him as a child, *he,* nonetheless, chose to accept those values (although he could not have chosen anything else) and it is *his* continuing subscription to those values which is tormenting him. In the simple sense that in the absence of anyone else's knowing of his homosexuality (other than his sexual partners), *he alone is his mental torturer.*

This is precisely what Daniel will not face, however. Which is not to say that he can simply decide, in an access of "liberated" thinking, to ignore the values he has internalized and which have been the basis of his entire sensibility for all his life. He can, however, start to *fight.* He is more than sufficiently well educated to know that other societies have not only tolerated but institutionalized homosexuality, and that some sectors of the educated middle and upper classes in his own society are well aware that homophobia is merely an irrational prejudice (witness his sneering at Mathieu, which we have just quoted, when the latter has this very reaction to the confession of his homosexuality). He can begin, in other words, by striving to free himself from the habit of allowing his conscience to be the docile instrument of his torment by conventional opinion. No doubt this would be not only be difficult and the work of many years, but such an enterprise would

quite probably prove only partly successful, so tenacious are our earliest influences. At the very least,
however, he would no longer need to have recourse to
the solutions we see him resort to in the book.

Not unlike Ivich, however, Daniel finds certain failure easier to choose than the uncertainties of a prolonged and difficult struggle for success. For instead
of revolting against his oppressed condition, Daniel
makes the fatal mistake of trying to go over to the side
of his oppressors: he tries to identify with the internalized Other, the cruel alter ego which possesses him (in
the old theological or demonic sense) and join his tormentors in their persecution of him—like those play-
ground failures and whipping boys (Woody Allen, for
example) who make a career out of turning themselves
into laughingstocks *before* the mob turns on them in
order to preempt and control the inevitable violence
they are usually subjected to. This identification can
never, of course, be completely or successfully achieved
because Daniel is simultaneously the victim of the tyrannical internalized Other. Furthermore, because
this elusive phantom represents his heteronomy, his
alienation to the project of the Other, and therefore by
definition cannot be the goal of his authentic freedom,
these frantic thrashings around only cause him to sink
deeper into the morass where he already finds himself.
For example, the bizarre decision to destroy that which
is most precious to him—his cats: here he has conceived the hope that perhaps if he could punish himself
sufficiently for what he feels to be a disgusting perver-
sion, he would suddenly *become* the tyrannical social
convention or alter ego which belabors him, make it
his own, *his* project, and spin free like a deranged sat-

ellite from the gravity of his own repulsive personal identity once and for all.

Daniel's project is impossible, of course. (How can one really punish oneself *as someone else*?—One is only really ever one person, however contradictory and conflict-ridden one's personality.) And so inevitably Daniel finds himself standing bewildered and impotent on the banks of the Seine, having failed to drown his cats and despising himself for his irresolution. The same impossibility applies to his attempt to castrate himself. He *knows* he was insincere and was just fooling himself, that he never had any real intention of actually doing it (AR 356). These exercises are fundamentally dishonest because they constitute attempts to achieve the impossible in full knowledge of their impossibility.

Most important of all, these existential contortions are an attempt by Daniel to deny his own freedom. In order to evade the recognition that it is he who perpetuates his own torment by a submissive complicity with an oppressive social order, he must find a way of denying his own agency in the constitution of what he takes to be his identity as a disgusting and contemptible pederast. The failures to drown his cats and castrate himself have taught him that he cannot inflict violence on himself as if he were an Other, as if, in other words, he had identified completely with the oppressive alter ego and managed to suppress entirely his own subjectivity, his own freedom, in order finally to arrive at the stage where he could treat himself simply as an object and not as the subject which he inescapably remains. One cannot inflict violence upon oneself in the way in which one does so to someone or something else because one is always also the awareness which protests:

> He was all hard and unyielding and then, from underneath, there was a weak victim who begged for mercy. He thought, "It's strange that one should be able to hate oneself as if one were an other." That wasn't true, moreover: try as he might, there was only one Daniel. When he despised himself, he had the impression of detaching himself from himself, gliding like an abstract judge above a teeming impurity (AR 109).

This infuriates Daniel because while he can, if he so chooses, try to despise himself absolutely or try to inflict the most atrocious forms of violence upon himself, he is always brought face to face with the possibility of doing otherwise: he can choose to consider himself differently. This is precisely what the protesting little voice suggests to him, which is why he cannot drown his cats, why he cannot castrate himself or even despise himself as completely as he would like to when he realizes how insincere his play-acting is:

> "I knew I wouldn't do it!" ... What a wretched play-actor he was.... He wanted to disgust himself with all his might—he would never again have such a fine opportunity for doing so. "Bastard! coward and fraud: bastard!" For a moment he thought that he would manage it, but no, these were just words. He would have had to—Ah! anyone, any judge, he would have accepted any judge but not *himself,* not this atrocious self-contempt which was never strong enough, this weak, feeble, moribund contempt which seemed on the verge of vanishing at any moment (ARS 356–57).

This feeble inconsistency of his self-loathing is the defining characteristic of Sartrean existential freedom: the fact that the mind never possesses the consistency of a *thing* or object; to be a subject is always to escape oneself, to be fleeting, inconsistent, indeterminate, eternally open-ended, never one's own object, never definitive, never frozen into one identity or meaning. The result is that Daniel's sado-masochistic conformism begins to develop the following phantasy as a new possible solution to his intolerable condition:

> To be what I am, to be a homosexual, a mean type, a coward, at last this filth who cannot even manage to exist. . . . To be a homosexual, in the same way an oak is an oak (R 133).

This is the motivation behind the otherwise inexplicable confession to Mathieu of a personal secret Daniel considers shameful:

> And then, now that there is someone who *knows,* I . . . I will perhaps manage to believe it myself (AR 390).

The attempt to identify with what Sartre, in *Being and Nothingness,* called one's *being-for-the-other*—our being as we appear to other people, as opposed to how we appear to ourselves—is an act of extreme desperation on Daniel's part, for he has been tormented all his life by the internalized gaze of the Other which he senses as inquisitorial, searching out his despicable secret:

> "It's frightening to see things for what they are," Daniel thought to himself. He imagined Hell to be like that: a gaze which would penetrate everything,

one would see to the end of the world—into one's very heart of hearts (AR 109).

He cannot even support the gaze of his favorite cat. The effort to see himself as the Other sees him, to identify exclusively with his being-for-the-other, is simply one more attempt to avoid the reality of his own subjectivity, to evade the fact that his own subjectivity is an accomplice of his tormentors: for he can only really see himself being seen by others. His freedom is always involved: *he* has to decide what to do with the way in which he is seen and judged by others. There is no way out. Furthermore, he can only play this trick on himself—the trick of trying to identify with his being-for-the-other while pretending that he has no part in the process—when in the presence of someone else, and specifically someone to whom he has confessed his guilty secret. For all these reasons Daniel will eventually be driven to a religious conversion—what for Sartre is the ultimate willful alienation of one's existential freedom to an external authority which is nonexistent and simply a delusory palliative for one's fear of assuming complete responsibility for the meaning of one's life. The eternal, omnipresent, and above all *absolute* witness which is God is what Daniel requires to remedy the merely relative and unsatisfactorily impermanent status of a witness like Mathieu:

Under the blue heaven, a bitter plaint, a vain supplication, *Eli, Eli, lama sabacthani,* these were the last words he encountered, they rose like light bubbles.... Open, open, the husk bursts, open, open, fulfilled, myself for eternity, homosexual, mean, cowardly. They see me; no. Not even that: *it* sees me.

He was the object of a gaze ... which condemned him to be himself, cowardly, hypocrite, homosexual for eternity.... But by whom? "I am not alone," Daniel said out aloud (R 135–36).

In the following crucial passage from the letter Daniel writes to Mathieu describing his religious conversion, we find Daniel's entire existential dilemma and its religious solution perfectly encapsulated:

Will you understand me first of all if I tell you that I have never known what I am? My vices, my virtues, they are under my nose, but I cannot see them, nor stand far enough back to view myself as a whole. And then I seem to be a sort of flabby and shifting matter in which words are engulfed; hardly have I tried to describe myself, than already he who is described is confused with him who describes and everything is put in doubt. I have often wanted to hate myself—you know that I had good reasons for doing so. But that hatred, as soon as I tried to apply it to myself, it drowned in my insubstantiality.... I understood as a result that one could only get to oneself through the judgment of an Other, through the hatred of an Other.... It was then that the most improbable and the most insane good fortune befell me. God sees me, Mathieu; I feel it, I know it.... What anguish to discover suddenly this gaze as a universal milieu from I could not escape. But what repose, as well. I at last know that I am. I am adapting for my own use and to your greatest indignation the imbecilic and criminal dictum of your prophet, the "I think, therefore I am," which has caused me to suffer so much—since the more I thought the less I seemed to be—and I say: I am seen, therefore I am. I no longer have to endure the responsibility of the insubstantial formless flow of my existence (R 405–07).

Here, in the final sentence, we have it, what for Sartre is Daniel's ultimate motivation for his conversion: he wants to abdicate from the responsibility of his own consciousness, his own freedom, the Cartesian *cogito*—the "I think, therefore I am." For it is precisely the insubstantiality of consciousness, for Sartre, the fact that it can never define itself conclusively—that, in short, one is always free to start all over again, to put everything in question—which makes us human, which *is* freedom, and which constitutes responsibility.

Daniel's religious conversion is highly idiosyncratic, tailored solely to his own existential needs. When we next encounter him, in *Troubled Sleep,* he is wandering around the deserted streets of Paris on the day the first German troops arrive to occupy the city, engaged in some remarkably un-Christian behavior: he is rubbing his hands with glee at the humiliation of France at the hands of Nazi Germany. Paris having been deserted in the face of the impending arrival of the enemy troops by the solid, worthy citizens whose homophobia Daniel has internalized, he walks the city all day long, feeling for the first time that this is *his* city, taking possession of it, feeling free for the first time in his life. Not surprisingly, this man who has felt himself to have been in a state of permanent internal exile within his own society now welcomes the conquerors, deriving an intense sexual pleasure from the spectacle of the handsome blond young Germans entering Paris:

Something crashed to the ground from the sky: it was the Ancient Tables of the Law! Fallen the society of judges, the sentence had been lifted.... "What freedom!" he thought, and his eyes grew moist. He was the sole survivor of the disaster. The only *man* before these angels of hatred and fury, these exterminating angels whose gazes upon him were restoring his childhood to him.... They are going to do Evil to us, it is the reign of Evil which is beginning, Paradise! He would have liked to have been a woman to be able to throw flowers to them (TS 105–06).

It is noticeable that Daniel has by now abandoned all thoughts of God. The reason is simple: the German army has freed him from the need for this concept by liberating him from the internalized gaze of French society. The change in his attitude to his own sexuality is immediate: when, in the course of this walk around Paris he first encounters the beautiful young Philippe Grésigne, his spontaneous reaction in the face of his own desire for the boy is initially dread, as the old familiar, trained, dutiful, horror of his self-loathing asserts itself. But then he remembers that "France is fucked," (TS 153), and so "anything goes" (TS 153).

Sartre clearly intended this new liaison to be a step on Daniel's path to freedom. Having enticed Philippe back to his apartment, Daniel observes him admiring a Mexican portrait of a dead child he has in his possession:

Philippe contemplated with ecstasy the portrait of the beautiful pale and disdainful child who returned his gaze from beyond the grave with all the self-assurance and the gravity of an initiate. "They look just the same," thought Daniel. Both blond,

both insolent and pale, one this side of the picture
and the second on the other side, the child who had
wanted to die [Philippe is contemplating suicide
from a bridge on the Seine when Daniel encounters
him] and the child who was really dead gazed at each
other (TS 164).

Because we have read earlier that the occupation of
Paris by the Germans restores to Daniel his childhood,
the suggestion is that the portrait of the dead child is
emblematic, both to Daniel himself and to the reader,
of Daniel's lost childhood. Furthermore, because on
this very day when he regains his childhood he encounters the youthful Philippe and saves *him* from suicide,
and because Philippe appreciates the portrait and
Daniel considers that Philippe and the dead child
resemble each other, it is fairly obvious that we are
intended to see Philippe as Daniel's opportunity to
rebuild his own life through what he can do for
Philippe:

> "I'll help you," thought Daniel with passion, "I'll
> help you." He wanted to save Philippe, to make a
> man of him. "I'll give you all that I have, you will
> know all that I know" (TS 161).

Philippe will be, in a sense, the resurrection of Daniel.
For example, he projects for him possibilities that he
had never been able to undertake for himself: "'You
will have to start by liquidating all values,'" he said
in a tone of joyous exaltation (TS 169). It is true that
this kind of talk is part of Daniel's seduction technique; but it is clear that this is also part of a projected
vicarious liberation of Philippe from the thrall of his
family. It had always been precisely Daniel's problem,

133

after all, that he had not been able to free himself from the conventional values he had internalized.

Unfortunately, this is the last we see of Daniel in the published volumes. What we do know of his ulterior development as recounted by de Beauvoir is that Philippe enters the Resistance in order to prove he is not a coward, and dies; Daniel, who has made good on his promise to collaborate up to the hilt with the Germans, crazed by grief attends a meeting of top German officers with a bomb concealed in his briefcase and blows himself and the Germans to pieces. Sartre seems here to have intended a demonstration which he would successfully carry to completion in *Saint Genet* and *The Devil and the Good Lord:* that neither the embrace of saintliness (or God, in the case of Daniel) nor the embrace of evil (Daniel's collaboration with the Germans) constitutes a viable solution to the aporias of human existence.

F. Further remarks on freedom

Before passing to a historical and sociological account of the novel, it may be well to clarify further the Sartrean notion of freedom. It will be recalled that both Daniel and Mathieu are obsessed with the relations between thought which is spontaneously engaged in activity and the self-reflective gaze of introspection which tries to turn around upon itself and make thought its own object. Daniel, for example, as we have seen, hopes to suppress self-consciousness itself in order to leave the nonreflective mind behind, undivided by the introspective gaze, having the satisfying unity and substantiality of a *thing:*

Imbecile! ... Above all, I should no longer watch myself, if I watch myself I become two. Be ... Be a homosexual, in the way an oak is an oak.... Extinguish the internal gaze (R 133).

Faced with the inherent impossibility of this exercise, he hits upon the solution of trying to identify with his being-for-the-Other, his appearance in the gaze of others, because other people as we view them from the outside as bodies, as physical objects, present us with the illusion of not being afflicted with the schizoid insubstantiality which is the subjective experience of consciousness from which we suffer ourselves. As we saw earlier, Daniel's religious conversion is an attempted solution to the problem he considers his homosexuality to be; but the conversion is also a solution to the problem presented by consciousness in its very internal structure, as we saw in his letter to Mathieu.

For Sartre, as Daniel's letter implies, it is in the very insubstantiality and elusiveness of thought that our fundamental freedom lies. Precisely because thought never becomes an object, or a thing, but is a constant movement and self-transformation which cannot ever truly become its own object because it is always necessarily implicated in its own self-examination and thereby creatively engaged in and responsible for both the act of introspection and the "object" of its own self-examination—for this reason thought is free and escapes the determinism of the scientific laws governing the interaction of physical entities. Descartes's celebrated dictum, to which Daniel alludes, would be more accurately stated, from Sartre's point of view, as *Cogito ergo non sum* (I think, therefore I am not). Precisely because consciousness is *nothing* (*no thing,* not even an immaterial soul), but merely a capability which emerges from the body as an ability to negate everything or set itself apart from everything in a perpetual creation of temporality—creating the past by distinguishing itself from its own past actions and straining toward the future which it projects before itself as a function of its own goals—we are free and thereby *responsible.* For this reason Daniel's refusal of the insubstantiality of consciousness (or "existence," as Sartre prefers to call it) is a refusal to assume the burden of his freedom.

Mathieu, for his part, is engaged in a diametrically opposed strategy: he likes to think that he is completely free, that he is nothing but freedom; whereas freedom, consciousness, existence, or whatever you choose to call it, however insubstantial it may be, is always a *commitment* which produces effects in the world that are all too material. Mathieu refuses to face either those real desires which are his free choices (for example, he wants to leave Marcelle and would in fact have been kinder to her had he accepted this and frankly expressed it at the outset instead of letting her discover the fact) or the very substantial social reality which his free choices have created for him and the responsibility they entail:

I was unable to take the money. My freedom is a myth, ... a nothingness, the proud and sinister dream of being nothing, of always being something other than what I in fact am. It's in order not to be my real age that I play around with these two brats; in vain: I'm a man, a grown-up, it was a grown-up, it was an established man of the world of work and adulthood who kissed little Ivich in the taxi. It's in order to try and escape from my social class that I write in the left-wing journals; in vain: I am a bourgeois, I was unable to take Lola's money, their taboos intimidate me. It's in order to escape from my life that I screw everything in sight, with Marcelle's permission, that I stubbornly refuse to get married; in vain: I am married, I live a domestic life (AR 282–83).

The constant failure to confront what he is in fact consistently choosing by each and every one of his actions—his desire to break off his relation with Marcelle—means that even introspective examinations of his own motives are just one more form of evasion. For example, while explaining to Boris why he resists drunkenness, he catches himself trying to make himself appear attractive to Ivich by citing a time-worn catch-phrase from Pascal ("I am a thinking reed") in what he hopes will be an interestingly ironic, world-weary tone:

He added ironically, as if to himself:
  "I am a thinking reed."
  As if to himself. But this wasn't true, he wasn't sincere: in reality he wanted to make a favorable impression on Ivich. He thought, "So, this is what I've come to?" He had got to the point of trying to exploit his downfall, he was not above extracting some small advantage from it, he was making use of it to engage in elegant conversation with young women. "Bastard!" But he stopped, taking fright: when he called himself a bastard, that wasn't sincere either, he wasn't really indignant. It was a ploy to redeem himself, he thought, to salvage his abjection

through "lucidity," but this lucidity didn't cost him anything, on the contrary, he was enjoying it. And this judgment he was passing on his lucidity, this manner of climbing onto his own shoulders.... "I would have to transform myself to the very bones" (AR 220).

Mathieu has begun to realize that the "lucidity" on which he has always prided himself is, as Marcelle had claimed, mostly just another subterfuge. Once one has decided to flee one's real existence by taking refuge in a futile relationship, one cannot hope to redeem the situation by any amount of lucidity about one's motives: one should just get up and leave. This is not something one needs to *think,* or ratiocinate, about in the way that Mathieu has adopted as his habitual modus operandi: one just *does* it.

Mathieu finally comes to this realization in *The Reprieve* when he undergoes something like a veritable conversion to freedom not unlike Odette's. He has been vegetating for months in the meaningless debris of his former existence as Marcelle's lover when he is mobilized. The imminent war changes Mathieu's relation to his own past: he had always lived in the expectation of a life lived in conditions of peace; the sudden realization that he was in fact destined to go to war makes his past even more laughable and absurd than he already considers it to be. The result is a transformation in his relation to himself:

There had once been a kindly, rather diffident man, who loved Paris.... This man was now dead.... He had been engulfed in the world's past, with the

Peace, his life had been entered in the archives of the Third Republic; his daily expenditures would provide material for the statistics of the standard of living of the middle classes after 1918. . . . A humble and mortal history: the war had crashed upon it and crushed it. . . . He opened his hands and let go; it took place deep inside him, in a region where words no longer have meaning. He let go, only a gaze remained. An entirely new gaze, without passion, a mere transparency. "I've lost my soul," he thought with joy (R 350–51).

The loss of his soul he refers to is really just the abandoning of his old habit of always trying to analyze himself as *something*—a soul, an ego, a "personality," or whatever—and the assumption of freedom which is mobilized at a level "where words have no meaning." There follows, over the next few pages, one of the finest and most vivid evocations of existential freedom in the literature of the period. Mathieu gazes across the street, from the terrace of the café where he is sitting, at the church on the opposite side of the street, and realizes that even if it is destroyed by a bomb the following day, even if he reverts to his former habits, nothing can take *this* moment from him:

Nothing can take from me this eternal moment. Nothing: there would have been, for ever, this dry flash lighting up the stones under the black night; the absolute, forever; the absolute, without cause, without reason, without aim, . . . gratuitous, . . . magnificent. "I am free," he suddenly said to himself. And his joy immediately turned into a crushing sense of anxiety (R 352).

Freedom, however, as this passage already implies, is not necessarily much fun. He wanders on through the streets of Paris:

In the middle of the Pont-Neuf he stopped, he started to laugh: "This freedom, I looked for it far and wide; it was so close to me that I couldn't see it, I couldn't touch it, it was in fact I myself. I am my freedom." He had hoped that one day he would be filled with joy, transfixed by a thunderbolt. But there was neither thunderbolt nor joy: simply this sense of destitution, this vertiginous emptiness in the face of himself, this anxiety which his own transparence prevented from ever seeing itself.... "I am nothing, I have nothing.... Freedom is an exile and I am condemned to be free" (R 362–63).

Partly out of despair at its emptiness, partly simply in order to toy with his freedom, to feel its vertiginous power, he comes within a hair's breadth of flinging himself into the river in a suicide attempt, but does not go through with it because suicide makes no more sense than life itself and it "would have just been a test" (R 364). In a second moment, a few pages further, he is at least able to recognize that he has been true to his childhood desire to be free and need no longer be ashamed of himself before the memory of the child he once was:

"I have not lost my childhood." The age of maturity, the age of reason, had disintegrated, but his childhood remained, warm and alive: he had never been so close to it. He thought once more of the little boy, lying on the dunes of Arcachon, the boy who had demanded to be free: in the face of that stubborn kid, Mathieu had ceased to be ashamed (R 376).

Finally, by the end of *The Reprieve,* demobilized with the temporary respite gained for Europe by the Munich agreement, he wonders with some perplexity what he will do with his civilian life. He refuses to return to his previous mediocrity and is heartened by the recollection of his newly won freedom:

He turned around abruptly; he looked smiling at the windows sparkling with sunshine. He felt strong; there was deep inside him a little stab of anxiety which was becoming familiar to him, a little stab of anxiety which gave him confidence . . . He no longer possessed anything, he was nothing. The somber night two days ago would not have been in vain, and this enormous upheaval would not be pointless. "Let them sheath their swords, if they want to; whether they have their war or whether they don't have it, I don't give a damn; I'm not taken in. . . . I shall remain free," he thought (R 444).

The final section of *Troubled Sleep*—which is devoted to Brunet's captivity and which is the only important part of the trilogy we have not discussed at any length—is relatively straightforward. We have already devoted enough commentary to it in the opening pages of this chapter to be able to proceed now directly to an account of *Roads to Freedom* as historical phenomenon.

II. Existentialist Freedom as a Utopian Transformation of the Functional Individual of Modern Industrial Capitalism

A. The Rise of the Modern Individual and the Existentialist "Cogito"

We have now achieved a certain understanding of the trilogy at one level: that of the work as an organized whole in which all the parts relate to one another such that any one part is visibly related to all the others and to the whole as it relates to each part. Each part derives its meaning from its interaction with the rest of the totality, and each part contributes toward the enhancement of the total meaning of the rest, much as each facet of a diamond reflects the light from all the other facets in the gem in an endless interplay of reflections without which the diamond would not achieve its brilliance. In just such a way any work of art achieves what we call "beauty" when a particular effect has been aimed at and then attained by the successful integration of all elements into the total project of accomplishing the effect in question. When we say, for example, that a work of art is a failure—in the sense that it is botched, rather than in the sense that we personally do not like or approve of the aesthetic effect or project aimed at—what we generally mean is that one or more elements do not *fit in* smoothly with the total project.[12]

Another way of putting all this is to say that up to now our aim has been to try and examine the work on its own terms: that is to say, we have sought to identify the traces of Sartre's own aesthetic project, his own *intentions* as he has tried to integrate every element of the work into a perfect signifying whole which would solicit a very specific response on the part of the reader.

Now despite considerable prejudice against this kind of analytic method in contemporary literary critical circles, there is in fact nothing wrong with it as it stands. It is, however, inadequate for real literary understanding; and indeed, insofar as something closely related to this method was for many years, under the label of New Criticism in the world of Anglo-American letters, practiced in isolation from other considerations, it was both deluded and mystifying to the extent that it assumed that people (or, at least, great writers) *really know what they are doing*. Whereas in fact we mostly do not. Not in the sense that we are all incompetents, but in the sense that all we do depends not only on extraordinarily complex social conditions of possibility (of which most of our actions are generally merely prolongations), but also in the sense that the real meaning of our actions cannot be reduced either to the subjective intentions which underlie them (which are, it must be emphasized, nonetheless real material events to be taken perfectly seriously, whatever their inadequacy for full understanding) or to the immediate consequences which are their result. I shall try and illustrate all of this by suggesting, at least some of the conditions which would have to be fulfilled if we are, as our title claims, really to understand Sartre.

For example, we reached the point where we have been in a position to suggest answers to such questions as, "On the basis of what aesthetic considerations does

Sartre introduce a character like Boris?" or, "Why is Mathieu obsessed with Ivich?" We have answered questions like these in terms of Sartre's project to demonstrate various possible ways of handling what he believes to be our existential freedom and the concomitant temptations to avoid confronting the burden of the responsibility of that freedom. But how about a rather different kind of question: "Why does existential freedom become the central preoccupation of a number of major writers and philosophers in the mid-twentieth century, and why does their work meet with tremendous success with the reading public?"

We can hardly claim to "understand Sartre" if we are unable to provide something of an answer to this kind of question; and, clearly, such questions cannot be answered without going beyond considerations of the personal intentions of the author or the exigencies of the internal aesthetic organization of the works in question.

We can start with the most visible problematic of the novel: that of freedom. What is distinctive about this issue as it appears in Sartre's work is that, unlike earlier formulations of the problem—as in the work of nineteenth-century French novelists like Stendhal or Balzac, for example, where it is a question of the lone individual striving for some form of freedom in the midst of a corrupt and conformist society which crushes the life out of him/her—here we are faced with a problematic which turns primarily around the relations of the individual with herself or himself, rather than an opposition between the individual and other people or "Society." As we have seen, freedom for Sartre in the trilogy consists in the recognition that consciousness, or the *cogito* (Descartes's "I think"), *is* freedom and can either be embraced as such or evaded by the individual. Furthermore, the freedom of the *cogito,* or conscious subject, consists in *its not being anything at all* and in its being *absurd*—that is to say, being bereft of any sanction other than its mobilization by itself in the pursuit of goals the legitimacy or illegitimacy of which it alone decides.

We have already, in our account of *Nausea,* examined some of the historical reasons for the rise of a historically novel situation where innocuous everyday objects could become susceptible to being perceived as grotesquely and monstrously absurd. The reasons for the appearance of the absurd *cogito* are closely related. In premodern societies—medieval feudal societies in Western Europe or so-called primitive societies elsewhere, for example—Descartes's idea that one might exist because one thought would have been utterly remote and alien. That the person's sense of personal identity and existence might have depended first and foremost upon a unique and distinct apprehension of the world and, above all, of oneself as an irreplaceable *individual* who was the sole arbiter of the meaning of the world in, as we say nowadays, "the pursuit of freedom and happiness" (i.e. the way in which the average modern person still in large measure sees him/herself today)—this lived understanding of what it is to be a human being and this way of *being* a human being would have been very strange to such older societies. Most historians associate the slow formation of the modern individual with the rise of capitalism in the interstices of the medieval feudal world; and the appearance of Descartes's *cogito,* or the Cartesian subject, in the early seventeenth century is generally taken as an indication that the modern individual was already in large measure formed by this time.

The Cartesian subject would prove to be a functional necessity to the new capitalist society which was in the process of being formed. Feudal society, for example, had functioned on the basis of extremely rigid social hierarchies and social arrangements where people knew their places and the behavior expected of them, where people's sense of their personal identity and the meanings of their lives were indicated for them by the complex networks of fealty and dominion binding serfs and lords, laypeople and clerics. Furthermore, at the ideological level, the social order was sanctioned by and integrated into an equally complex and carefully ordered cosmological order which arranged all the levels of life (animal, human, and so on) in relation to a divine order of the creation which included angels and the Christian God.

A social order of this kind is completely incompatible with capitalism. Imagine what would happen to modern industry if the majority of workers were suddenly bound to rural overlords (or, indeed, anyone—even an industrial capitalist) by oaths of fealty, the breaking of which might entail death. Capitalism can only function on the basis of the vast majority of people being able to do whatever they choose (within the legal bounds of the preservation of private property, life, and limb) except not spend the best part of their lives working for someone else. This principle functions at all kinds of intimate levels of everyday existence in apparently innocuous ways which we take for granted. Capi-

146

talism could not exist, for example, if social values (moral, aesthetic, or whatever) were to remain fixed and rigid over long periods of time as in a primitive or traditional society. We can once again take the example of fashion used earlier in the chapter on *Nausea:* if all Americans were to wear their consumer products out completely before discarding them, instead of purchasing new ones which are more fashionable (and thereby experienced as really being more attractive than their predecessors), the country would be plunged into a severe economic depression. For fashion to work as it does, people have to accept that there exists no *one* style, no *one* form of beauty—that bell-bottom jeans may have been attractive in the 60s and early 70s, for example, but could no longer be so in the late 70s, and yet can be brought back as one option among many in the 80s as a form of "retro" nostalgia for a bygone era. And, of course, fashion of this kind is a preeminently modern—very recent, historically speaking—capitalist product. Even today in India, a country which has undergone many of the convulsive changes which the introduction of a modern capitalist economy brings with it, it is still possible for a grandmother to pass on a sari to a grateful granddaughter without there being any sense of a "generation gap" in the two women's conceptions of what constitutes an attractive garment.

Now, the kind of extraordinary human flexibility and adaptability which is demanded by fashion is necessary for the functioning of capitalism at *all* levels of social existence. As is well known, capitalist industrialists exist in a state of constant competition with one another: in order to survive, each capitalist has to try and produce a commodity which can be sold for a price that is at least as low as that of the principal competitors. To do this means having constant recourse to the latest technology which will reduce costs by producing more commodities in less time and with less labour. But new technology always introduces changes in social institutions. For example, industrial capitalism destroyed the traditional extended family of several generations sharing the same home by taking economic production out of the household and organizing it in factories around heavy machinery on the sole basis of local conditions of supply and demand. (The massively increased demand for social mobility this entailed is one of the reasons why compulsory education was introduced—one's grandmother, who traditionally might have taught one to read, for example, now lives across or out of town or has been placed in an Old Age Home). Now that our economy is rich enough and the new kinds of jobs being created by an increasingly services- and information-based economy are ideally suited to being performed by women (the kind of women our societies had been traditionally producing), capitalism is now in the process of eliminating the nuclear family in its turn—the latter constituted by a working father and a mother who raises her children and performs all necessary domestic labor.

This kind of world, which requires endless transformation of all social institutions, of all values, of nature, of the very kinds of people we are as we have to adapt to the constant changes in our society—this kind of world demands that, if one is to survive in such a world, one be an individual who is ideally utterly bereft of any fixed identity or determining characteristics—for example, someone bound to any geographical region, any value system or life style—beyond a limitless capacity for adaptation. In reality, of course, such individuals are rarely met with; but movement in this direction has certainly been the overall tendency of changes wrought in the individual over the last few centuries. The one constant feature in world history during this period—and which distinguishes the modern period from the rest of history—has been an ever-accelerating process of change, in the course of which traditional belief or value systems and social institutions across the entire globe have been either annihilated or radically transformed. We have already evoked, in our account of *Nausea,* the massive process of secularization of the world, the "death of God," which was one dimension of this process of change, and the immense changes it has wrought in our perception of the most banal everyday objects.

Sartrean existential freedom simply represents the most extreme version of, and logical conclusion to, this development. Which is not to say that Sartre's work is to be viewed merely as a passive reflection of social and historical forces beyond the author's control. On the contrary, Sartre's work can only be fully comprehended as a vigorous attempt to manage, to come to terms with, the new kind of human reality which had been solicited and produced by a new age. For it is perfectly clear that no social order that has yet existed could really afford to produce citizens endowed with the degree of real freedom and autonomy of thought which Sartrean existential freedom mobilizes and not disappear in a revolution. Indeed, Sartre, along with many other writers, artists, and musicians of the modernist avant-garde of the twentieth century, was un-questionably in part responsible—in the indirect and delayed, or secondary, way in which art can be said to contribute to social change—for the social upheavals of the 1960s which were, in large measure, a mass expression of the social demands implicitly or explicitly formulated by artistic modernity in general: greater acceptance of sexuality which was neither exclusively heterosexual nor conjugal, the liberalization of dress codes, the acquisition of abortion rights, and a broad demand for "freedom" in all domains.

What had happened in effect was that in the course of producing the new individual which capitalism required—someone who was endowed with far greater autonomy than any preceding social individual—a genie had been inadvertently let out of the bottle: the very individual which had been produced as a necessary functional component by a certain kind of society turned around upon its master-creator and demanded its abolition. On the whole, after some initial fumbling and attempts at outright repression, capitalism responded to the crisis with great flexibility and skill. The utopian demands unleashed in the 60s were tamed by these demands being met at the level of private space. Sexual freedom, a generalized sensualisation of the everyday lived, a loosening of codes of dress and body language, and a watered-down, commercialized version of the most dangerous demands of the 60s were *sold* to the protesters—without any of those concessions in the political and economic domains which would have made for fundamental change being met. Thus, if urban life did not exactly become a carnival, at least you could listen to superb stereo renditions of heavy rock music on the tape deck of your BMW or on your Walkman. With the wisdom of hindsight it is possible to see that there is absolutely nothing surprising in the yuppie phenomenon's following hard upon the heels of the hippie movement: without fundamental change at the level of the major economic and political institutions which determine the shape of the overall society, yuppies—who enjoy and take for granted all the freedoms at the level of private space or private life style which hippies had had to fight for—have been successfully bought off and tranquilized by the blandishments of consumer society. Yuppies are simply hippies who are unabashed about making money.

One should be careful, however, about representing the tranquilization of existential freedom undertaken by consumer society as assuming merely the form of a crass materialism. This process is effected at many levels of daily existence which are so discreet as to be subliminal. One has only to think of the extent, for example, to which music has invaded our daily lives. For the existentialists, silence and solitude were always the privileged occasions for the sudden brutal and unnerving experience of freedom to break through the reassuring banality of what Heidegger called "everydayness." Music constantly piped into our daily lives—in elevators, banks and supermarkets, or via boom boxes and Walkmans—defuses the immediate anxiety of choosing the meaning of one's life by setting a tone, a mood, which provides the meaning prepackaged, to which one can abandon oneself, without really *listening* to the music. (That would require a mobilization of resolute freedom which most of the music in question strenuously discourages, being expressly de-

151

signed merely to keep one in a state of permanent semidistraction from the life of higher vermin that most of us lead.) Television, of course, notoriously fulfills a similar function. To sit in one's living room and have to drag the resources for living out of the kind of exhausted, bored, vacuous state of mind that functional adaptation to this world requires is so much more difficult than flicking the remote control and having a plot, a story line (*meaning,* in short), brought into one's life with reassuring regularity at the same time every day or every week. To do something oneself requires one to set objectives, to totalize the world or form the entire world with its varying coefficient of resistance around those objectives into something which closely resembles a literary plot: "If I do this, then such and such a thing may happen, and I will be able to ..." A single television image, as the advertising artists have discovered, can tell an entire story in one image. (Always along the same lines: "If you buy product X, you will at last be happy." This implicitly recognizes and thrives upon the fact that everyone is already unhappy precisely because of the abysmal quality of life in a world which has only these forms of satisfaction to offer!) And our deciphering of the image is effortless. Nonetheless, the terrible fear of freedom persists, and is still not considered to have been safely neutralized. After all, one might just conceivably stare at a television image in the wrong way—as Roquentin stared at the chestnut tree in *Nausea*—and so it is extremely rare to find images on television that are not accompanied by a musical background to set the tone, to make quite sure that one does not get out of line and start getting ideas of one's own. Thus it is increasingly unusual, for example, to see a nature program that does not feel compelled to excise the wonderful silence of the African savannah—a silence in which the rare bird calls, insect sounds, and intermittent passing of a breeze over the tall grass constitute half the awful beauty of the landscape—by maintaining a reassuring trivial jangling in the background. This even affects "high" cultural programs: about five years ago a British production of *King Lear,* starring Laurence Olivier, could not be shown to an American public without a fourth-rate imitation-Mahler accompaniment such that much of Shakespeare's text was inaudible.

B. Why Marxism?

This brings us to the next major question. The issue of existential freedom in the trilogy is inextricably bound up with a political agenda. Both Brunet and Mathieu attain a Sartrean ideal when they become activists in political movements committed to the transformation of society by violent change (while retaining, nonetheless, an intellectual autonomy which makes their commitment always provisional). Mathieu's progression from disengaged intellectual, through the discovery and assumption of existential freedom, to political activism is clearly intended to have didactic force. What then is the relation between existential freedom, or the *cogito,* and communist revolution, and why should they figure as intertwined in Sartre's trilogy? After all, is there not an apparent contradiction in the idea of a conception of freedom as aggressively individualistic and nonconformist as Sartre's joining forces with an ideology we have frequently had represented to us as the acme of mindless gray conformism and political tyranny? These questions also impinge on the wider issue of Sartre's choice of World War II, and the clash of the world-historical titans—fascism, communism, and the parliamentary democracies—which constituted that conflict, as the backdrop to this work.

In order to understand Sartre's embracing Marxism, and the qualified support he expressed for the Soviet Union up to 1956 when the Soviets invaded Hungary (he had, however, always refused to join the French Communist Party), it must be recalled that from the end of the Second World War until roughly the end of the 1960s, Marxism, as a body of theoretical knowledge and as an instrument of social and philosophical analysis, enjoyed enormous prestige among French writers and intellectuals in general. The Soviet Union itself (frequently distinguished sharply by Western Marxists from Marxism as a theory and instrument of knowledge or inspirational source of political practice) had enjoyed a similar favor since the 1920s which it only really decisively lost in 1956. The Bolshevik Revolution of 1917 had been widely hailed throughout Europe as a new beginning for humanity in the aftermath of World War I, the latter conflict having represented for many the moral, cultural, and political bankruptcy of the ruling classes. Throughout this period socialist ideology made substantial inroads among the Western European working classes and intelligentsia. At the end of the Second World War the Soviet Union emerged as having borne the brunt of the conflict and having played far and away the major part among the

Allies in the defeat of Hitler. Likewise, the French Communist Party had been the dominant faction in the French Resistance to the Nazi occupation of France, whereas much of the French political Right had been discredited by collaboration with the occupiers. For such reasons, and many others, the French Communist Party would be for many years the largest political party in France, although never able to form a governmental majority in the National Assembly. Sartre, like many other French intellectuals of the period, despite the existence of the prison camps in the Soviet Union (which he denounced), gave the Soviets and the French Communist Party his qualified support on many issues.

None of this suffices to explain, however, the apparent confluence between existential freedom and Marxism for Sartre. On reflection, the two are scarcely incompatible. Just as the Cartesian *cogito* and its more extreme version, Sartrean freedom, were the products of, or possibilities inherent within, a capitalist social existence, so Marxism—as Marx himself pointed out— was itself a possibility contained within capitalism. The basic impulse in capitalism, after all, is the rational mastery of nature (with the assistance of capitalism's "handmaiden," modern science—the latter inextricably bound up with the historical rise of the former) with a view to the total commodification of the planet in the name of profit. Marxism simply expanded the control of nature to include the rational social control of history: to the extent that the latter was viewed as being merely the sum product of the actions of millions of individuals, a collective rational organization of history would have as its ideal consequence that

155

instead of being the victims, or objects, of history as a vast bewildering process beyond our control, we would become the *subjects* or agents of our own history. Instead of there existing an irreducible tragic difference between our individual desires and projects, on the one hand, and the iron historical realities, on the other, which since time immemorial have always thwarted and limited our desires, humanity would be able to *choose* its destiny through miracles of social engineering which would mirror and surpass our recently acquired control of nature. The appeal that a social program of this kind would have had for Sartre is obvious: it enables Sartre/Mathieu to choose his own destiny without such a choice being the merely irresponsible individualistic simplification of individual and social reality which Mathieu had evinced at the beginning of the trilogy. Both individual destiny and the great opaque swirling vortex of world history—the enigma of which, as it is experienced by the individual participant and spectator, is one of the central preoccupations of the trilogy—would ideally be comprehended and *lived* by the light of one single vision and concrete destiny. Mathieu's early, primitive, wish to choose his own life independently of anyone else and his growing awareness of the need to, and his desire to, transcend this trivial and futile individualism in a great collective adventure—both these countervailing desires would be resolved in one great novel synthesis.

It is here that the legacy of Hegelian thought becomes most visible in both Marxism and the work of Sartre. Hegel defined freedom in the following manner: "We become free when we are confronted by no absolutely alien world, but depend upon a fact which we ourselves are."[13] In other words, one is free, according to Hegel, when one only deals with oneself; when, in a blaze of mystical illumination, one has attained a level of awareness where one comprehends that the totality of being is oneself and one is oneself the totality of being. In its Marxist-existentialist, demysticized, shrunken, Sartrean version, one attains true freedom through solidarity with the collective socialist project of the liberation of humanity. Alternatively, one can *evoke* freedom of this kind at the aesthetic level. What is *The Reprieve*—with its proliferation of characters among whom the narrative line switches back and forth in an effort to evoke the simultaneity of the same historical event in different people all over Europe— what is *The Reprieve* if not an evocation of freedom through the novelist's playing God and putting the reader in the position to feel fleetingly that he or she is God? (This is true in the sense that the novel presents the war as one coherent process which—even if no one other than God can really comprehend it and God does not exist—is nonetheless a totality of human freedoms of which it is the outcome and which can, at least aesthetically, be *imagined*).

As late as the 1950s, when Khruschev had denounced Stalin's atrocities at the Twentieth Congress of the Communist Party and he appeared to be launching a campaign of liberalization within the Soviet Union, and before the invasions of Hungary, Czechoslovakia, and Afghanistan would definitively disqualify the Soviet Union in their eyes—many intellectuals the world over could still find Marxism an appealing doctrine.[14] All the more so to the extent that the great and unprecedented blossoming of Hegel studies (in

157

France) in the 1930s and early 40s, led primarily by Alexandre Kojève and Jean Hyppolite, had prepared fertile ground for a massive proliferation of writing inspired by the discovery of Marx's very Hegelian 1844 manuscripts, published in Moscow for the first time in 1932, which would dominate French intellectual life from the 40s down to the end of the 50s. The very Hegelian (at least on one reading of Hegel), "humanistic," notions like "alienation" and "reification" in these early texts of Marx and the writings of the great unorthodox Hungarian Marxist Georg Lukács, who also exerted a tremendous influence in this period, dovetailed very neatly with French existentialism. Alienation, for example, refers to that process whereby the traces of human activity accumulate and acquire an inertia or momentum of their own such that they come to stand over against the original human agents as a hostile force which may well produce a result the exact opposite of what was originally intended. Thus, when a worker goes into the job market she, with the millions of others in her position, unwittingly contributes to the lowering of demand for her own labor power and a depression of her eventual wages. (The same applies to capitalists competing for a share of a market; the price of their commodity drops.) The successful implementation of communism would, ideally, lead to the elimination of this kind of gulf opening up between intention and historical consequence. Instead of being a haphazard accumulation of millions of individual projects acting independently of one another, which would confront humanity as an uncontrollable, incomprehensible, and hostile force crushing all before it, history would become the transparent, rationally controlled medium of human intention. The parallel with Sartrean existentialism is clear: just as in Marxism the redemption of history is achieved by its being recognized as, and then perfected as, the collective outcome of human activity, so in existentialism consciousness can only achieve authentic freedom when it assumes the freedom *that it is.*

This confluence of Marxism and existentialism is an important dimension of the trilogy at levels other than those we have already examined. For example, Sartre suggests at a number of points in *The Reprieve* that it is the French bourgeoisie that is opposed to standing up to Hitler over his territorial demands on Czechoslovakia because it is afraid that such a war would eventually lead to a left-wing revolution in France (R 14-15) and the continental hegemony of the Soviet Union in the event of a victory by France and Britain over Germany (R 209). (The former fear could well have been realized: one of the very first tasks the deeply conservative General de Gaulle had to set himself upon assuming power after the liberation of France in 1944 was the disarming and dispersal of the communist Resistance groups.) In effect, the view was widely held in prewar Europe that the only dependable and substantial force standing between Hitler and world domination was communism. This was the justification, for example, which double-agent Kim Philby gave for his betrayal of Britain; and it was the reason most frequently cited by the volunteers from all over Europe who flocked to join the republican side against the fascist General Franco in the Spanish Civil War. To many the Western bourgeois democracies, with their spineless temporizing with Hitler, seemed suspiciously ready to give Hitler a free hand, hoping against hope that he might even be tempted to do for capitalism what the invading British, French, German, Polish, Japanese, and American armies had been unable to do when they intervened in the civil war which followed the Bolshevik Revolution: destroy communism. The frequently execrated nonaggression pact signed by Hitler and Stalin only days before World War II could easily be understood as Stalin's riposte to the dangerously exposed situation which the Munich agreement had left him in (a riposte as cynical and ruthless as the Munich agreement itself insofar as it freed Hitler to move against Western Europe and therefore must be held to have been one of the direct causes of the war). Against this background there is surely a deliberate didactic parallel established by Sartre between Chamberlain's desire to gain time for British rearmament for a later conflict with Hitler by sacrificing Czechoslovakia, and the characterization of Mathieu early in *The Age of Reason* where he is described as having failed to commit himself to life because he is keeping himself available for some great occasion in the future (AR 64).

C. "Public" History vs the "Private" Individual: Sartre as Critic of the Modern Nuclear Family, and Herald of its Disintegration

The implication is that Mathieu's refusal to commit himself to an active role in the political struggles of the day is in effect to align him with the forces of bourgeois reaction whose ambivalence toward Hitler contributed to the eventual conflagration of world war, the humiliating defeat of France, and the four-year Nazi reign of terror over occupied Europe. The point is reinforced by Gomez, the painter turned revolutionary general in the Spanish Civil War, when he talks pointedly to Mathieu about the French "[who] are not involved and [who] don't know what's going on, they are just afraid" (R 266). He is referring to the French government, but by extension the French in general and Mathieu in particular—the French who have failed to intervene forcefully on the side of justice and freedom and so will eventually pay the price for their refusal to stand up to facism in Spain by having to face it on their own soil.

We have examined in detail above Mathieu's conversion to political activism and his slow realization—one that mirrors Sartre's own political radicalization— that he, like anyone else, is necessarily already implicated in an ineluctably political situation and that even inaction is a form of commitment. What needs to be examined now, if we are truly to understand all this, are the historical conditions which gave rise to the sudden emergence of this entire problematic in the literature of the mid-twentieth century—a problematic which is, after all, historically novel.

The problematic depends on a distinction between what we continue today to call *private* life and *public* life—say, Mathieu's love life involving Marcelle and Ivich, on the one hand, and his sudden and unexpected participation in the destiny of France as a soldier, on the other—a distinction which the trilogy finally suggests is erroneous. Some idea of how tenacious our thinking in terms of this distinction is, and how provincial we are (from a broad historical point of view) in subscribing to this distinction, can be gained by briefly considering our reaction to the explanation for the cause of the Trojan War that is provided by Homer. It will be recalled that according to *The Iliad,* Paris, the son of the Trojan king, abducts the beautiful Helen, wife of Menelaus, brother of the Mycenaean king Agamemnon, carrying her off to Troy. The mobilization of the independent Greek cities around Agamemnon, the launching of the great armada of ships to carry the Greek forces to Asia Minor, the terrible siege of Troy which lasts for years, the frightful losses endured by the Greeks before they finally prevail—all this is undertaken simply to avenge this affront. I don't think it would be an exaggeration to say that the modern reader finds this implausible. Charmingly quaint, no doubt, but nonetheless preposterous. Today the idea of a great affair of state like warfare being subordinated to a domestic trifle of this kind is grotesque.

It would be a mistake to assume that this implausibility is a function of naïveté on the part of Homer. Homer is (whether as oral tradition or more or less independent scribe) one of the greatest literary artists of the Western tradition. The explanation for what can appear to us as a gross flaw must reside in this explanation's having been perfectly plausible to Homer's Greek audience. In other words, the distinction we draw today between domestic or private life and public affairs of state—the distinction around which Sartre's trilogy turns as an explicit attempt to subvert and demystify it—had nothing like the same force for the Greeks that it has for us today. The distinction scarcely existed for the Greeks because public and private were inextricably intertwined in the social arrangements of a small-scale agricultural society, where marriage was an occasion for the exchange of property (of which the woman herself might be one of the objects) and the forging of political alliances. This attitude toward an occasion that we today would see in terms of "love" is not an irrational barbarism which we have transcended because we are now miraculously more enlightened or more "civilized." In agricultural societies where manual labor is the primary source of energy women and children were, and continue to be in many parts of the world, crucial ends both to survival and, eventually, to wealth and power. It is a simple fact that one person cannot successfully cultivate a plot of land except in extraordinarily favorable circumstances. Similarly, children in such societies are insurance policies for old age when the state, as we know it today in the West, does not provide this kind of insurance. Reasons such as these continue to be the most important obstacles facing birth-control programs in rural China today.

It can easily be imagined how, in these circumstances, politics and domestic existence are one. The two domains only really begin to become distinct when money, rather than land or women, becomes the primary source of wealth and power, in other words, only really in the post-Renaissance period. As recently as the sixteenth century Elizabeth I of England could not marry—either an English nobleman or a foreign monarch—because if she did, she would no longer be able to play off the great continental powers against each other as they sought her hand in marriage. The sixteenth century provides us with an example that will make the changes which have taken place especially vivid. In Shakespeare's history plays—especially in the cycle of *Henry IV, Part I* through *Henry V*—we find the first signs of the split between private and public existence which is so familiar to us today. The most visible theme of these plays is the young Prince of Wales's resolution of the tension that exists between the competing demands of his official role as heir to the throne (his "public responsibilities") and his penchant for revelry and irresponsible escapades with his drinking-companions, (his "private" existence, which is finally ruthlessly abandoned and subordinated to the exigencies of governance and statecraft). This dramatic distinction between the demotic world of the tavern or brothel, on the one hand, and the stage of "world history," on the other, heralds our familiar contemporary divide between "the people" and "politics" (the "history" of our high school textbooks, limited to accounts of kings and battles). This divide did not exist in premodern, preurban, societies. By the early nineteenth century, however, it is firmly established, as can be seen in the novels of Sir Walter Scott, where history becomes an extraordinary adventure in which the individual becomes involved through some fortuitous accident of fate. The divide between public and private will achieve its most intense expression with the twentieth century in the work of Kafka: in *The Trial* the main character is arrested and finally executed on charges which are never made clear to him by a government agency whose existence and motives remain completely enigmatic to its victim. In Kafka's work the connection between the private individual and the collectivity has become so tenuous and mysterious that existence itself acquires the strange unreality and inconsequentiality of a dream.

There are two paramount reasons for the historical appearance of a radical divorce between private and public life. First, throughout the period dating from the Neolithic revolution (the moment, approximately ten to fifteen thousand years ago, when we learned to domesticate animals and sow crops, enabling ourselves thereby to produce surpluses of food that could permit the rise of social classes which were not directly involved in production and could be freed from this labor in order to perform other specialized functions) we have slowly increased our production of food and wealth to the point we have reached today, where we are able to sustain vast populations of which only a small fraction are involved in the production of food. (Even as recently as this century the number of Americans involved in agriculture has continued to decline dramatically.) This advantage and the fact that our modern urban societies are tremendously complex and require constant administration have led to the growth of highly specialized classes of people engaged full time in this administration—politicians, bureaucrats, and officials. Second, modern industrial capitalism—which gradually became the dominant form of economic production in the West from, roughly, the late eighteenth century until the mid-1950s—took work out of the home and organized it in factories and offices where it could be performed with heavy machinery and under strict disciplined control (in order to maximize production). This led increasingly to a perception, historically novel, of home and work as two distinct spheres.

Home—increasingly during this period built around the nuclear family of a working father and a mother who stayed at home and reared her children (at least, for the middle classes—most black women in this country, for example, have always worked)—became a utopian space of privacy, "love," etc., secluded from the brutality, alienation, and monotony of the "outside world" of work. This explains the historically unprecedented importance attached to romantic love in our culture. Love is constantly represented to us as the secular equivalent of religious salvation (fulfilling a function closely related to that of art in the modern age, as we saw in chapter 2), often taking precedence over all other moral or worldly considerations and without which one's life is considered worthless or a failure. That other ages and cultures have taken a very different view of the matter is vividly illustrated by the example of Dante, who consigned the great lovers of history (Paris, Tristan, Cleopatra and company) to the second circle of hell.

This was a revolution in sensibilities because, for most of human history, work and the family (mostly extended) had been inseparable. Even when, in the early stages of industrial capitalism, huge numbers of women and children were employed in factories and mines in dangerous and insalubrious conditions, this was not always opposed by working-class people because it enabled families to remain together on the job. As the tremendous social costs of these arrangements became apparent (deterioration of the health of the work force, for example, and thereby its capacity to produce profit, or the impossibility under these circumstances of the education of children), and as the complexity of industrial society and its economic activity grew, and increasingly a productive work force required at least the fundamentals of literacy and elementary computation, the now familiar system of compulsory education for children and women being relegated to the role of housewife (initially only for the middle-classes and then, increasingly, as an ideal to which more successful sectors of the working-classes could aspire) gradually fell into place.[15]

That the entire structure of the family had been subordinated primarily to someone else's economic production, and that this nuclear family structure was not much fun to live in, soon became evident. Freud's work would be a direct product of the nuclear family, showing how this extremely impoverished structure—deprived of the rich range of emotional resources and alternatives of the extended family—was a fiercely competitive and incestuous enclave, a veritable hotbed of neurosis and unhappiness for all concerned. Already by the mid-nineteenth century, the French literary avant-garde (Flaubert, for example) was portraying the bourgeois family as characterized by an inevitable tedium and mediocrity to be relieved only by fitful bouts of marital infidelity.

The view that marriage, as we have understood it in recent times, is a uniquely bourgeois institution, a form of economic and sexual servitude, is constant in the tradition of the French novel from Flaubert down to Sartre. In the trilogy only two marriages are portrayed among the principal characters: that of Ivich (which we do not see, but we are assured that it is a disaster) and that of Jacques and Odette, in which the latter is clearly oppressed. For the rest, not a single main character is married. The book's attitude toward the institution of marriage is best characterized in the following conversation between Daniel and Mathieu:

"As a matter of fact," he said, "it can't be so very disagreeable to be a fuck-up. I mean a complete fuck-up, finished. A guy who's married with three kids, as you say. It must have a real calming effect!"

"It certainly must," said Mathieu. "I meet guys like that every day. Parents of pupils, for example, who come to see me. Four children, their wives are unfaithful to them, members of the Parents' Association. They seem quite calm. I would even say benign."

"They have a kind of gaiety of their own, too," said Daniel. "They give me vertigo. And you, that really doesn't tempt you? I can just see you married," he continued, "you would be just like them, overweight, neatly dressed, telling the right jokes at the right moments, and with celluloid eyes" (AR 124).

It is perhaps worth mentioning at this point that Sartre himself never married. His lifelong companion, Simone de Beauvoir, tells us in her autobiography that they had made a pact early on in their relationship (the terms of the agreement seem to have been dictated primarily by Sartre) that they would remain together for the rest of their lives without marriage or cohabitation, and that both would remain free to take on other lovers. (At one point Sartre did offer to marry de Beauvoir so that they could get teaching posts in the same town, but she refused.) Both parties stuck to the pact. The arrangement has been variously assessed as either an admirable example of great fidelity and loyalty within freedom, or a case of gross egotism on the part of Sartre.

The assault on marriage and the nuclear family in the trilogy, then, has to be understood as part of the broader attempt to transcend a narrow individualism which rigorously separates the private world of the family from the public domain of "history" or the "outside world." While Sartre does manage convincingly, I think, to demonstrate that individual behavior always has macrohistorical consequences (Mathieu's abstention from political engagement makes him the accomplice of the fascist conquests of the Second World War), his own historical moment is such that he is not yet in a position to demonstrate that politics and economics are at work within the family itself—that marriage, for example, is always a political and economic act, that the division of labor within the household is political and economic. This demonstration would be the historical mission of post–World War II feminism, in which Simone de Beauvoir would play a founding role.

The assault on marriage is also, however, a function of individualism to the extent it represents one more dimension of coming to self-consciousness of the freedom of choice, and absence of rigid social identity, in the modern individual. This vastly augmented freedom of choice available to the individual is, of course, impossible without the enormous increase in economic productivity which has been possible under capitalism. In premodern societies, for example, for a man not to be able to marry, or to refuse to get married, was always either a major personal misfortune or an act of antisocial irresponsibility, because the individual in question would not be able to provide for himself without the labor, initially of his wife or wives, and then that of his children, becoming thereby an economic burden on the rest of his extended family or the wider community. For this reason bachelors were more often than not objects of scorn and social neglect. For the same reason, homosexuality—except in certain special circumstances (where there was a chronic shortage of women, for example)—was almost universally fiercely proscribed in premodern societies, and continues to be subject to intense homophobic prejudice in most Third World societies today. These examples help us get a sense of the very special historical conditions in which the challenge to marriage, or the representation of homosexuality as a condition to be freely assumed in the face of social stigma, could appear in *Roads to Freedom*.

Sartre's generalized assault on the nuclear family and the institution of marriage should not, however, blind us to the fact that he necessarily falls under the sway of certain of their effects at a number of points. Thus, for example, the women he portrays in his works are all very much, as we might expect, the products of these institutions as they existed in the world in which he wrote. Sartre's women are all what he would describe elsewhere, in his philosophical works, as "relative beings"—that is to say, people who are not sovereign subjects, exercising their own freedom, but people who are in the final analysis agents whose activities consist in the implementation of the projects of others (men), passive agents if you will. This is not to suggest that women in Sartre's works do not often occupy positive roles—roles which effectively criticize masculine existential modes. In the trilogy Marcelle would be a case in point as we have seen earlier. However, despite her hostility to marriage and a settled bourgeois existence, Marcelle remains very much what the French call *une femme d'intérieur*—a woman of the home. Thus, she scarcely ever goes out, confined to her room by a mysterious malady which, because it is never explained or described as anything other than a more or less constant unwillingness to confront the outside world, smacks of hysteria or housewife depression. Such activity as she does engage in is always in reponse to the initiatives of men, Mathieu and Daniel, whose innocent victim she becomes. Indeed, unlike the men of the trilogy—and like the other women characters (Lola, Ivich, Sarah)—she appears to have no *future,* that masculine prerogative par excellence, the practical domain which is projected out of busy activity. She disappears mysteriously from her husband's side without explanation on Sartre's part when Daniel suddenly reemerges in Paris as the Germans enter the city. The lives of all Sartre's women characters seem to be subordinated to men in this manner. The rather "mannish" and ostensibly independent Anny in *Nausea*—who no longer believes in or expects anything from "love"—exits from the novel on the arm of, and supported by, a wealthy young playboy figure. Hilda, in *The Devil and the Good Lord*—who serves as the positive pole in the play, representing the possibility of a human existence which is based on love, equality, and reciprocity and which is not alienated to the inhuman ideal of religious belief—is, at the end of the play, hovering around the male hero, Goetz, in a nursemaid/mother role, waiting for him to come to his senses and accept the love she offers him. Even the virago militant, Olga, in *Dirty Hands,* betrays an incapacity for masculine activity by botching an assassination attempt, closing her eyes at the last moment in anticipation of the noise of the explosion and thereby missing her target.

D. Concluding Remarks

It only remains for us now to determine the degree to which Sartre has been successful in his attempt to show the artificiality of any separation of private life and world history. I think it would be generally agreed that the demonstration is successful in the case of Mathieu Delarue. It is possible to raise some doubts, however, about the aesthetic viability of *The Reprieve.* The proliferation of minor characters which are not meaningfully related to one another (except implicitly to the extent that all of them are participating in the preparations for the war) is a weakness. Of course, it was precisely Sartre's intention to illustrate the immense dispersion of the historical process and the impossibility—unless one were God—of discerning the fundamental historical unity of these divergent threads. The incoherence is deliberate up to a point. Many readers, however, have found it tedious. Perhaps this is simply because the ultimate unity of these distinct lives—the totality of history itself—is something that cannot be demonstrated in a novel but is more appropriately the domain of political economy, sociology, and history. (Even Tolstoy, when he sought to show in *War and Peace* that the great clash between France and Russia in 1812 was not the emanation of the wills of two individuals—the Emperors Napoleon and Alexander—but the outcome of all the millions of individuals who participated, was only able to do so at the level of discursive arguments rather than at the level of the characters he depicted.)[16] This inherent limit in the realist novel as a literary form means that, in *The Reprieve,* a switch from one character to another is always initiated in order to show what is going on elsewhere; and it is always announced, or eased into, by a deliberate similarity in, or analogy between, the situations of the respective characters. Thus, at page 223, for example, we switch suddenly from the crippled Charles being lifted on a stretcher into a train to the lately deceased Monsieur Viguier's body being lowered into his grave. This is all very well as a technique of novelistic coherence and intelligibility; but from a strictly Marxist point of view (a yardstick against which it seems perfectly fair to measure a Marxist novelist) it must necessarily fail to demonstrate the fundamental structural unity of the historical process in question—a unity which, as we have suggested, it is probable that only a properly historical analysis could display. Mere temporal simultaneity and similarity in theme or situation come across as merely *empirical*—not *necessary*—historical unity. The result is an inevitable superficiality and triteness because the mode of these transitions adds nothing to our understanding of the war. In short, Mathieu/Sartre's assessment that one would need "to be everywhere at the same time" in order to understand the war, that one would "need to be God"—impossible for Mathieu, but at least partially realized as an aesthetic ideal by the author/reader in *The Reprieve*—is itself an inadequate requirement for historical understanding. What mitigates this weakness, on the other hand, are those moments where Sartre successfully establishes real links between the behavior of his characters and the war as their final outcome—Mathieu's abdication from political responsibility as a miniature version of the Western democracies' appeasement of Hitler, for example, or the opportunism and cowardice of the French and Western European bourgeoisie (Jacques) in the face of Nazi aggression. But this kind of *necessary* unity is not sustained as consistently and successfully by Sartre as his great predecessor, Balzac, managed to do in such novels as *Lost Illusions* and *Splendors and Miseries of the Courtesans,* in which his establishment of the links between plot and character masterfully depicted the fundamental nature of the new society which had replaced the *ancien régime*. (One could make the same unfavorable comparison with Stendhal.)

With Sartre's trilogy we see literature straining at its very limits. Sartre's remaining literary production after the trilogy will deepen the investigation of the problematics first developed in this work in ways that are often fascinating, but it will not transcend the limits of a certain kind of literature. In this respect it heralds the end of literature as we had known it up to that point in time. The next wave of writers to achieve acclaim in France—the first writers of postmodernity: Beckett, Robbe-Grillet, Duras, Tournier and others—would do so by writing novels that are frequently works "to the power of two": that is works which interrogate and subvert earlier forms of literature and their means of representation far more overtly and at a far more fundamental level than anything modernism has come up with. This tendency in its most extreme form—in the work of Beckett—seems to imply that literature can only continue by demolishing itself in ever more extreme statements of nullity. Far from being a purely negative phenomenon, however—a merely apolitical nihilism (as Beckett's work has on occasion been represented) or an arid formalism (Sartre would level this charge at Robbe-Grillet)—literary postmodernism is first of all a tribute to Sartre's generation: a certain kind of literature could not be improved upon, had been played out, and was therefore an exhausted vein. Secondly, and more importantly, these works often sought to demonstrate within their own literary texture that literary conventions (plot, character, etc.), the very instruments of literary representation—indeed, representation itself—are always preeminently political and ideological acts. None of this can detain us here. Some pointers to the reasons for this major shift in literary practice are provided in the final section of chapter 4 below.

NOTES

1. This is perhaps the main reason why *Nausea* is the only one of Sartre's literary works to have achieved the status of literary classic, always given pride of place in literary histories of the period and endlessly prescribed for undergraduate courses in French literature of the twentieth century.

2. There was to have been a fourth volume, *The Last Chance,* of which we possess two complete chapters and some notes and drafts. Sartre abandoned the novel in 1949 when he came to feel that the historical conjuncture of the postwar era had evolved to the point where the starkly simple issues of the war—e.g., to collaborate or not with the German occupation of France—were no longer pertinent

in the more complex and ambivalent circumstances of peace time. The contents of this fourth volume, such as we know it, are summarized below.

3. It should be pointed out that this translation of the French title, *La Mort dans l'âme,* is inappropriate (the French means literally "death in the soul"); it was more accurately translated by an earlier English version as *Iron in the Soul.* The question is not without importance, as the French expression used in the title comes up at a number of points in the novel and clearly sums up both the defeat of France and Mathieu's experience of it as it puts the finishing touches, as it were, to the futility of his own private life.

4. The controversies raging within feminist scholarship at the moment mean that it is possible to adopt two very different attitudes toward the phenomenon described in this section. Thus, the contestation of what is historically an older bourgeois "centered" conception of the individual in the very terms in which it is revised—through a "feminization" of the individual—can be seen from the perspective of a feminism which contests any "essentializing" version of the *masculine* or the *feminine* into timeless innate *sexual* dispositions (rather than socially constructed *gender*) as retrograde in its very attempt to undermine male dominance and a "phallogocentric" version of human activity. On the other hand, there exist strands of feminism which aggressively assume those existential modes traditionally encoded as feminine as indeed specifically feminine (without quotation marks), or *female,* and which argue, moreover, that these feminine existential modes should be actively promoted and valorized as such as a corrective to the millennial discriminatory valorization of masculine existential modes. Sartre, I would suggest, holds gender to be a social construct and, in the trilogy, promotes androgyny as a positive alternative to traditional gender roles; but not the variety of androgyny which has been criticized by some feminists as the ideology of that "bourgeois feminism" which merely entails the acquisition of traditionally masculine existential qualities—autonomy, competitiveness, a capacity for "rational" decision-making, and so on—by women in the interests of the adaptation of women workers to a male capitalist workplace. An adaptation which takes place without a critique of masculine rationality and patriarchal socioeconomic arrangements (a useful account of these debates can be found in Hester Eisenstein, *Contemporary Feminist Thought* [Boston: G.K.

Hall, 1983]). As will be seen, androgyny, for Sartre, constitutes an interrogation and critical reevaluation of masculine modes of existence. It must be said, however, that this critique seems only to entail a feminization (and fresh empowerment, thereby) of men (Mathieu and Brunet). Only an incipient (and future) virilization of women (in the sole case of Odette) is implied. In this respect, Sartre only goes some of the way beyond analogous earlier feminizations of male protagonists in French literature, in Romanticism, e.g. (see Margaret Waller, "*Cherchez la femme:* Male Malady and Narrative Politics in the French Romantic Novel," PMLA, 104, [March 1989] 141–51).

5. E.g., Sigmund Freud, *The Interpretation of Dreams* (New York: Avon Books, 1965), esp. chapter VI, "The Dream-work."

6. Recent work by feminists has exposed the manner in which these notions of Freud gave expression to and helped perpetuate sexism, but simultaneously made possible at another level the eventual demystification of the sexism implicit in Freud's own theoretical constructs and the social phenomena he was describing. Much has been written on this subject, but see especially Luce Irigaray *This Sex Which Is Not One,* trans. Catherine Porter with Carolyn Burke (Ithaca: Cornell University Press, 1985), *Speculum of the Other Woman,* trans. Gillian C. Gill (Ithaca: Cornell University Press, 1985) and Sarah Kofman *The Enigma of Woman: Woman in Freud's Writings,* trans. Catherine Porter (Ithaca: Cornell University Press, 1985).

7. In our culture the night is traditionally subsumed under the feminine principle, as is, of course, nature—which means that Sartre, despite an impulse to move beyond the phallic law, nevertheless still mobilizes the traditional oppositions of that law. See below for Sartre's choice of a forest as a backdrop to this scene.

8. Luce Irigaray, *This Sex Which Is Not One,* trans. Catherine Porter with Carolyn Burke (Ithaca: Cornell University Press, 1985).

9. Freud, 391.

10. *Nausea* 128, 133, 134. See my comments on these passages in chap. 2 above.

11. Simone de Beauvoir, *La force des choses,* (Paris: Gallimard, 1963) 212–14.

12. It should be mentioned that this conception of artistic production has been convincingly put in question by Marxist, psychoana-

lytic, and deconstructionist criticism: these approaches demonstrate that the perfect totality of the work of art is always necessarily undermined by unreduced residues which make this ideal in effect an unattainable ideal. This fact does not, however, contradict our assertion that it is with the assumption of a totality that artists work—even an avant-garde work of utter fragmentation has to operate a unification among its diverse elements in order to ensure that they cannot be subsumed under a unitary meaning (the writer makes sure that element A seems disturbingly gratuitous or inconsequential with regard to element Z etc.). Furthermore, one can only deconstruct, for example, a structure which presents itself *as* a totality (or an attempt thereat).

13. G.W.F. Hegel, *Lesser Logic,* trans. William Wallace (Oxford: Clarendon Press, 1975) 64.

14. Anyway, it was never difficult for Western Marxists to defend Marxism as having been betrayed in the Soviet Union, as Marx himself had never described a post-capitalist society (except in the vaguest terms) and had limited himself in *Capital* to analyses of capitalism. With the collapse, under Gorbachev, of a major obstacle to political change in the West—the bogeyman of communist tyranny in the East—the Marxist critique of a West that is as in need of *perestroika* as the East (misplaced triumphant posturing notwithstanding) will only intensify.

15. As these examples imply, for a Marxist like Sartre the entire apparatus of the modern state—from compulsory education through public health systems to national defense and institutions of law and order—exists not as a benign instrument for the welfare of the mass of citizens (as we are assured) but in order to assume, on the backs of taxpayers (the majority of whom are employees, not employers, and who not only provide the vast bulk of the state's revenues but are, relative to absolute income, those most severely burdened by taxation), the expense of the successful creation, preservation, and renewal of a healthy, docile, and sufficiently educated work force for exploitation by the owners of capital. The bridging of the divide between public and private life in modernity in Sartre's trilogy implicitly challenges, therefore, the legitimacy of the capitalist state (and, for that matter, the privileges of the Soviet state–capitalist bureaucracy which operates a similar mystification and oppression).

16. E.g., ch. 28 of volume 2.

CHAPTER FOUR

Theater

Some of Sartre's plays are relatively short; none of them has the density of works like *Nausea* or the trilogy. Also, there is a fundamental continuity running through all the plays, and the best-known and most successful ones can be dealt with in chronological order in a single chapter.

The Flies: Beyond the Oedipus Complex

The Flies is based on the *The Libation Bearers,* which is the second panel of Aeschylus's trilogy, the *Oresteia.* In large measure Sartre reiterates the essentials of his ancient Greek predecessor's cast and plot. Thus, the young Orestes, the son of Agamemnon, returns to his family's palace at Argos, the scene of his royal father's assassination at the hands of his wife Clytemnestra and her paramour, the usurper Aegisthus. He reveals his identity to his sister Electra and, with her approval, eventually avenges his father by slaying both Aegisthus and Clytemnestra. This outline apart, however, the two plays are radically different. A comparison between the two works will be helpful in determining Sartre's intentions and the significance of his play.

The Libation Bearers is but one episode in the unfolding triptych of dynastic murder, blood vendetta, incest, and intrafamily cannibalism which is the legacy of the ancient curse upon the house of Pelops, from which, according to the ancient Greek myth, all the principal characters are descended. Aeschylus is primarily concerned with the laying to rest of an interminably proliferating blood vendetta—it has embroiled four generations —and its resolution by submission to arbitration by a civic authority which transcends and suspends private vengeance in the name of the law of a third party, the *polis,* the Greek city-state. The immense contemporary popular success enjoyed by the depiction of such a resolution in the third panel of the *Oresteia—The Eumenides,* in which the case is tried by a tribunal of Athenian judges and in which the Furies of the title (who were the traditional avengers of crimes against the bonds of kinship) are assigned new functions by Pallas Athena—suggests that Aeschylus was enabling his public to recognize, and work through, a similar evolution in their own social arrangements: a new conception of the family, social law, and the body politic in line with the economic changes constituting the growth of the urban *polis.* (As we shall see shortly, Sartre too is engaged in both actively producing and understanding a major change in the nature of family relations.)

The emphasis of *The Flies* is quite different to the extent that, for Sartre, the drama of the action does not arise so much out of whether or not Orestes will succeed in avenging Agamemnon and in taking possession of his rightful heritage as it does out of the inevitable psychological tension which arises from committing an act of violence which is believed by the agent to be simultaneously a horrifying crime—matri-

cide—and a moral imperative—the justifiable avenging of victims and the restoration of the legitimate
political order. This element is a dimension of Aeschylus's play too, of course; but the crucial difference resides in the fact that, for Aeschylus, this conflict can
only be resolved by the intercession of a god, who de-
flects the Furies (the externalization and incarnation
of what we today would call conscience) into a new
function. For Sartre, on the other hand, human freedom is the only absolute and the only legitimate or
authentic legislator of the meaning and moral value
of human action. He is above all concerned to liberate
us from a conception of conscience or moral order
which is anything other than a *human* construction.
It may well be horrifying to kill one's mother, but once
one has decided that it is *right and proper to do so,* then
it makes absolutely no sense to feel *guilty* about it: to
do so would be to alienate one's freedom to a transcendental moral order, or god, which does not really exist,
and which even if it did exist—in the shape of Zeus,
as the play hypothetically, or for the sake of argument,
suggests—would have to be defied and would be power-
less in the face of human freedom anyway. Which is
in no sense, according to Sartre, to be heartless or callous about the acts in question. As Orestes explains to
Electra, he will bear the burden of the memory of his
mother's last moments for the rest of his days; but he
is damned if he will regret what he has *chosen* to do
and repudiate an act which he continues to believe was
justified. Remorse would somehow imply that one had
not acted responsibly in the first place, that one had
not taken the full measure of the horror of what one
was undertaking before embarking upon it, that one

was avoiding assuming full responsibility for what one had done. Thus it is that Orestes vanquishes the flies of Zeus and the Furies (Erinyes), which symbolize the alienation of the freedom of the citizens of Argos to their collective guilt at their complicity in the murder of Agamemnon. It is for this reason too that, after slaying Aegisthus and Clytemnestra he refuses to rule over Argos: for temporal power, according to the terms of the play, is only able to function by persuading a population to renounce its freedom and subordinate itself, tyrannized by its own guilty imperfections, to a moral order which is presented as an absolute —godgiven, not the merely relative product of human choice and devising—over and against the population in question and in whose name alone it is able to impose itself convincingly.

In interviews[1] Sartre explained the play—it was written and produced in 1943—as an attempt to counteract the efforts made by the collaborationist Vichy government to represent the defeat and German occupation of France as a deserved chastisement to which it should submit itself patiently, humbly, and passively. The play was intended (and widely interpreted as such by the French public) as an appeal to the country, thinly disguised in ancient Greek garb, to rise up against the occupiers. As Sartre put it, he wished to address the dilemma of "the terrorist who, by shooting down Germans in the street, provokes the execution of fifty French hostages."[2] In due course we shall see Sartre grapple with a similar dilemma facing the social revolutionary engaged in class warfare in two later plays—*Dirty Hands* and *The Devil and the Good Lord*. In both instances he will arrive at a conclusion similar to the one proposed here in *The Flies:* in the face of political injustice which can only be brought to an end by violent change, to stand by helplessly wringing one's hands, unwilling to sully them, is to act in bad faith. Furthermore, unless one *takes* one's freedom (as opposed to having it bestowed by others), one will never really be free: one cannot allow others to do all the dirty work. This is the moral Sartre intends by the example of Electra who, because she is not an entirely enthusiastic or active participant in the murders of the usurpers, will fall prey to the hounding, guilt-inducing Furies.

This historically local, topical, dimension to the play is certainly present. More fundamentally, and more enduringly, however, *The Flies* is an attempt to come to terms with and assume what Nietzsche called the "advent of nihilism"—that is, the necessary dissolution of all traditional (especially Christian) values and beliefs under the hammer blows of modernity, before the work of construction of a new and more vital philosophy would be able to confront that which Christianity and the other "degenerate" "slave moralities" had found unacceptable. Indeed, this dictum from Nietzsche's *The Twilight of the Idols* might have served as the perfect epigraph to *The Flies:* "Not to perpetrate cowardice against one's own acts! Not to leave them in the lurch afterward! The bite of conscience is indecent."[3] Sartre himself is keenly aware of the historically specific character of Orestes' conception of freedom, and has shrewdly supplied his hero with the necessary personal history to explain the otherwise anachronistically modern sense he has of the relativity of all beliefs and traditions, his distinctly modern lack of a sense of belonging which will make his impious crimes and exhilaratingly liberating absence of remorse a plausible existential possibility. As his tutor says to him early on in the play:

Didn't I make you, from early on, read all books in order to make you familiar with the diversity of human opinions, and make you visit a hundred nations, showing you in each case how human customs are variable? At present, here you are, ... liberated from all forms of servitude and all beliefs, without a family, without a motherland, without a religion, without an occupation, free for any kind of commitment and knowing that one should never commit oneself (F 61).

And Orestes will complain to Electra:

Who am I and what do I have to give? I hardly exist: of all the ghosts who roam today through this town, none is more ghostly and unreal than I (F 90).

Like so many of Sartre's male intellectual heroes—Mathieu in *Roads to Freedom,* Hugo in *Dirty Hands,* indeed, Sartre himself—Orestes will dream of redeeming his condition of being a free-floating, disengaged, debilitatingly skeptical and irresponsible intellectual without attachments by means of "an irreparable act" (F 94–95) which is preferably both violent and revolutionary. (Sartre is perfectly aware of the origins of this phantasy in social class: as the level-headed, ruthlessly pragmatic, communist militant Hoederer in *Dirty Hands* will say to the idealist bourgeois intellectual Hugo, in a tone of amused perplexity, "What a rage you all have for playing at being killers!") Certainly, as Orestes puts it, to belong to a place, to a community, one has to interact with it. In typically Sartrean fashion, however, Orestes feels obliged to have recourse to extreme measures; indeed, far from revenge being the overriding motive of his crimes, as in the *Oresteia,* Sartre's hero seems, curiously, to want to commit violent crimes primarily in order thereby to belong to his native community and, thus, to become *real:*

> My path . . . leads down to the town. I must go down, do you understand? go down until I reach you all, you are at the bottom of a hole, right at the bottom. . . . I am too light. I need to give myself ballast by means of a very weighty crime which will make me sink headfirst, to the bottom of Argos. . . . Come, Electra, look at our town, . . . it is for the taking, I have felt it since this morning. And you too, Electra, you are for the taking. I will take you all. I will become an ax; and I will chop in two these stubborn walls, I will open the belly of these overdevout houses, . . . I will become an ax and I will bury myself in the heart of this town like the ax in the heart of an oak (f 93).

Revolution has always been the quintessential founding act of modernity—whether at the level of social and political institutions or at the level of the economy, modern science, and all modern cultural production—in all three of which permanent revolution has been the sine qua non. Now, regicide is undoubtedly a revolutionary political act. However, we have already dealt in large measure with this dimension of Sartre's writing (his commitment to violent political change) in chapter 3, and we will return to it with

Dirty Hands and *The Devil and the Good Lord*. What should be noted and examined in *The Flies* is the *erotic,* or more precisely, psychoanalytic, dimension of the long excerpt quoted directly above: the assimilation of Argos to a woman to be "taken" aggressively, the description of the town as a "hole" into which Orestes must sink himself, and the comparison of the houses of the town to a stomach to be torn open and into which Orestes will bury himself like an ax being driven into an oak. All of this is unmistakably familiar imagery of aggressive male sexual possession. What is important about it, from our point of view, is that it is also Oedipal: not only is Aegisthus Orestes' stepfather, but he is also Agamemnon's cousin. For both these reasons—by means of what Freud called "displacement,"[4] and also because the king, not merely according to Freud, but according to millennial mainstream patriarchal discourse, is always also the father—for these reasons Aegisthus is a stand-in for Orestes' own father, Agamemnon. Furthermore, the motherland is always also, in terms of a similar displacement one's mother.

What is important about all this, however, is not that the play can be interpreted in these terms, as just another tedious mobilization of the Oedipus complex, but that the play represents an attempt by Sartre to go *beyond* the Oedipus complex and the nuclear family of which the Oedipus complex is simultaneously the mainstay and product. As such, the play is one more instance of Sartre's anticipation of, and militant involvement in, the major social changes which have taken place in the industrialized West over the last forty-odd years, changes which include the disintegration of the nuclear family and a contestation of patriarchy. In representations of the Oedipus complex which bow to its Law and endorse its premises (psychoanalysis, Sophocles) the young male who rises up against the father's possession of the desirable mother either submits to the interdiction of incest under threat of castration by the terrifying figure of the father or, in the exceptional event of parricide and incest with the mother, succumbs to the guilt provoked by the internalization of the law and then performs his own ritual self-mutilation, or symbolic castration, as a sign of his placing himself once more under the law. Thus Oedipus, in Sophocles' play, blinds himself upon discovering that he has unwittingly murdered his own father and married his mother. Likewise Aeschylus's Orestes cannot enjoy the fruits of his parricide and follow the injunctions of the chorus to rule over Argos—in psychoanalytic terms, possess his mother(land)—but flees Argos hounded by the guilt-inducing Furies. In *The Flies*, however, Orestes, having slain his father, not only experiences no remorse but spurns the throne of Argos as that which will perpetuate the tyrannical guilt-inducing law of the father (what Freud called the superego), which is ultimately that of the father of all fathers and king of all kings: Zeus himself. Zeus is all too aware of what is at stake, and for this very reason seeks to seduce Orestes into sustaining the patriarchal law by accepting the allurements of power, by occupying the place of the Father.

Sartre, in other words, in *The Flies,* as in the other works we have examined, is implicitly advancing a fresh conception of the family: one which is post-nuclear and post-Oedipal.[5] We know now that the misnamed "traditional" nuclear family (misnamed because it was primarily the invention of the modern age and displaced only very recently the older forms of the extended family, which really *was* "traditional") and the Oedipus complex, as Freud formulated it, were peculiar to the modern West.[6] It is also clear that the nuclear family and its attendant Oedipal conflict were the forcing house of the modern individual. Born of the competition between father and son (the normative individual of the modern age was consistently represented as male) for the affections of a single female figure (compare the richer emotional resources of an extended family of more than two vertical generations and the additional presence of collateral relations in the pre-modern village/settlement or nomadic hunter-gatherer group), and the competition among siblings for the limited attention of only two adult figures, the offspring of this singular arrangement was perfectly formed for his destiny of ferocious denial of sexual, emotional, and sensuous satisfaction (Freudian repression) in the interests of fierce competition and a single-minded devotion to hard work and the accumulation of wealth unprecedented in human history. (Estimates vary with the premodern society in question, but there is substantial agreement that even societies living in harsh environments devoted considerably less time to work—in some cases, as little as one half as much—than we do today.)

As we read *The Flies* today, in a context of high divorce rates, single-parent households, where gay rights are advocated, where abortion has been legalized in most of the Western world, and where patriarchy is on the way out with the growing emancipation of women, it is this post nuclear-familial dimension of the play—as it anticipates and solicits so many of these new social arrangements—which necessarily engages our attention, rather than its local historical pretext, the German occupation of France (the deeper level connection between Fascism, Oedipus, and the overthrow of the state indicated in note 6 above notwithstanding).

In this respect *The Flies* anticipates later plays like *Dirty Hands* and *The Devil and the Good Lord* in which a central preoccupation will be the critique of what Sartre calls "bourgeois moralism"—that is a conception of morality that is based on abstract, universal ethical principles (for example, honesty, justice, nonviolence) rather than a pragmatic assessment of what is feasible and best in an immediate and necessarily contradictory and violent political arena. To the extent that, according to Freud (whose theory applies strictly to the patriarchal nuclear family), it was the satisfactory resolution of the Oedipal complex by means of the internalization of the father's terrifying interdiction of incest with the mother, under the implicit threat of castration, which provided the seed of the male infant's conscience or submission to the moral law (his superego), *The Flies*—with its violent overthrow of the father and his moral law, and its refusal to accept the guilt attendant thereupon—not only participates in the progressive decline of the patriarch and the nuclear family which has marked the twentieth century as a whole but also opens the way to violent political revolution. In point of fact, however, the actual historical outcome of the contestation of the bourgeois nuclear-familial social order on the part of artistic modernity, and its offspring of the 60s, would be the "liberation" of, strictly, private desire in the form of consumerism and endlessly extended credit.

No Exit: Alienation under Capitalist Relations of Production

Three characters are locked up together in a drawing room in hell. It soon turns out (as one might have expected from an atheist) that this hell contains no torturers with cloven feet and horns wielding branding irons. The play is really an allegory about human relations under certain conditions: the three occupants of the room—as they realize to their growing horror—have been carefully chosen as the kinds of people best suited to be one another's infernal tormentors.

Estelle, a pretty, frivolous, narcissistic, and wealthy young woman, had got through her life by depending on male desire to found and legitimize her trivial vapid existence. Garcin had been a journalist fighting for the cause of pacifism. At the outbreak of war he had been arrested trying to cross the national border in order to escape military service and had been shot for desertion. He is tormented by uncertainty as to whether he was a pacifist by genuine conviction or simply a coward. The question is a burning one for him, as he had lived his life as a callous, misogynistic Don Juan deriving pleasure from breaking the hearts of his victims, at his happiest in a stereotypically macho milieu of sweaty male journalists in shirt sleeves smelling of cigar smoke. These characteristics are introduced by Sartre in order to suggest that Garcin needs to persuade himself that he is "a real man"—a fact which implies that he is probably right to have doubts about his moral courage and the sincerity of his political commitment: if these had not been questionable, then he would not have felt the need to play the role of a Don Juan or have recourse to a macho decor to persuade himself of his masculinity. Inès had been a young working-class lesbian—and a sadist. Like Daniel in *Roads to Freedom,* she is a sadist because she has internalized the disapproving gaze of a homophobic society which transforms her into a loathsome object. She says of herself, "I was what they call, down there, a woman damned" (NE 26) (the English translation erroneously gives "a damned bitch"), a conventional euphemism of the period for a lesbian. Her sadism represents an attempt to transform the Other into the ultimate object in his or her turn. In Sartre's view this is a fatal error as it means she has implicitly accepted the terms in which she is condemned by the society in which she lives instead of freely assuming her sexual preference. Like Garcin and Estelle she has alienated her freedom to her being-for-the-other. She is fatally attracted to Estelle, who, as a social snob and a woman who is utterly dependent upon an approving male gaze, by definition cannot reciprocate her desire. Estelle, for her part, predictably turns to Garcin, hoping to find salvation in his arms; but he can only love her on condition that she persuade him that she believes he is not a coward. Estelle, however, makes the fatal mistake—in part as a result of jealous provocation on the part of Inès—of betraying the fact that she doesn't give a damn one way or the other. Besides, under the hostile gaze of Inès, who is determined to believe that Garcin really is a coward, he is unable to make love to Estelle.

By definition incapable of giving one another what each one desperately wants, the trio have successfully constituted their own irremediable hell: "Hell is other people" (NE 47), as Garcin puts it in an oft-quoted and widely misunderstood conclusion to the play. This is *not* Sartre's definitive assessment of human relations. It is instead an anatomy of human existence when it is alienated to being-for-the-other—when one founds one's identity on the basis of how others perceive us and react to us, rather than in terms of the indefinable freedom which Sartre considers to be the ultimate truth of our condition (see chapter 3, part I, sections E and F above). It is this failure of the characters to assume their freedom (what Sartre, in *Being and Nothingness* diagnosed as "bad faith"), this failure to live independently of their being-for-the-other, which makes their hell an eternal condition. That this alienation to the Other is a free choice they have made is amply demonstrated by the fact that at one point the door to their chamber mysteriously opens, and they decide to ignore the possibility they have of leaving hell. Which is why the English title, *No Exit,* is a misleading translation of the French, *Huis clos,* which means "in camera," or a trial which is held behind closed doors, not open to the public. There is, in other words, a way out which the characters consistently refuse to take.

From a broad historical perspective—without this being a conscious dimension of Sartre's aesthetic project, but by virtue of the context in which the play was written and which it necessarily thereby implicitly comments upon—*No Exit* can also be read as a political and social allegory. It is an indictment of a society which, as an inescapable environment which sets up the terms for all human relations, pits all its members against one another: not just capitalists against workers, but capitalists against capitalists in their competition for markets (a competition which causes prices to fall and so works against this class as a whole) and workers against workers in their competition for jobs (which lowers wages):

> They've laid their snare damned cunningly—like a cobweb. If you make the slightest gesture, if you raise your hand to fan yourself, Estelle and I feel the vibrations. Alone, none of us can save himself or herself; we have to sink or swim together (NE 29).

This is a perfect diagnosis of alienation under capitalism as defined by Marxism and the latter's prescription for emancipation (see the section on *The Condemned of Altona/Loser Wins* and, especially, chapter 3, part II, section B).

It is only once capitalist modernity has destroyed the traditional social order we evoked in earlier chapters—in which the identity of the individual was established once and for all on the basis of her or his position in the society as a whole, which itself is ultimately sanctioned in religious terms—only once this order has been destroyed does the life-and-death struggle between free-floating autonomous individuals over their identities (for example, in Garcin's case, "Am I a coward or am I not?") arise in its unmistakably individualistic form—that is, in which one defines oneself or is

193

defined in moral, or sexual, terms rather than by one's place in the social organization. The historical novelty of this situation can be made vividly clear if we turn once again to Homer. In *The Iliad* the conflict which pits Agamemnon against Achilles in the opening book arises as a consequence of Agamemnon's affront to a priest of Apollo. The priest is the father of Chryseis, whom Agamemnon has taken as his concubine as one of the spoils of war. When the priest tries to regain his daughter by offering a ransom, Agamemnon drives him away with threatening words. Apollo spreads a plague among the Greek army, and Agamemnon realizes he will have to accept the ransom and return the young woman. But his role as paramount leader of the Greek host makes this an intolerable indignity to be suffered before his men, and he demands that one of the other Greek leaders compensate his loss with one of their female prizes. This is patently unjust, but nevertheless a demand which is an inexorable imperative of the dignity of his position without which he must necessarily lose face and see his authority as leader of the Greeks diminished: "Find me then some prize that shall be my own, lest I only / among the Argives go without, since that were unfitting."[7] Achilles, in his turn, as the foremost warrior among the Greek leaders, is the logical choice to be the one who will challenge Agamemnon on the subject. All the more so to the extent that—in this society based on carefully gauged degrees of rank, precedence, and military prestige—Agamemnon, if he is to retain his authority, must face down and take the concubine of the foremost among his men, Achilles, as that prize which—because of the prestige of her owner—alone can placate his wounded pride and sustain his authority. Achilles himself, no less bound by the irresistible logic of the etiquette of power and military prestige, must in his turn rise to the challenge, and duly does so, with all the well-known tragic consequences for the Greek expedition. The point of all this is that the reactions of the two men are generated solely by the imperatives of their social ranks, rather than the individual psychological characteristics in terms of which the conflict is generally explained by so much traditional commentary on Homer (Achilles' "pride" or "arrogance," and so on). The situation we are dealing with in *No Exit*—where the individual is faced only with a choice between mobilizing her or his existential freedom and alienating his or her identity to the other—is a very recent historical phenomenon. As late as the seventeenth century, in the works of the great French tragedian Pierre Corneille, inevitable tragedy is still being produced by the irreconcilable exigencies of the characters' social ranks.

Furthermore, only under capitalism, where all relations are defined by competition—notwithstanding instances of class alliances and class solidarity (trade unions for workers or cartels and trusts for capitalists, organizations that are explicit recognitions of and attempts to mitigate the competition between individuals), and notwithstanding the instances of personal friendship or romantic love which temper these institutional realities—only under capitalism are all interpersonal relations structurally or a priori defined at the very outset by competition. (This is not to deny that competition could exist in premodern societies—we have just seen an example of such competition in

The Iliad—but it was less pervasive and less universal.) Whereas in premodern societies (especially preurban premodern societies) individualistic competition for the necessities of life was always frowned upon for the simple reason that the survival of the individual and of the group—because of the low level of technological development—depended upon the cohesion and integrity of the group; which is why a kind of "primitive communism," as Marx called it, often existed.

The result of universal competition under capitalism is that human relations in this kind of a society are defined by hatred and violence to an unprecedented degree. This is especially evident in the United States, the most purely capitalist society we have yet seen (primarily because of the absence of the kinds of social and cultural legacies of earlier modes of production which one finds, for example, in Europe or the emergent Asian capitalist powerhouses). It is most obviously manifest in the massive involvement of the lumpen-proletariat of the ghettos in violent crime: armed robbery, gang wars over the lucrative drug trade etc.. These communities are merely accepting and implementing the logic upon which this society is founded. But the same phenomenon—and Sartre is conscious of this in *No Exit* as the *ne plus ultra* of capitalist social relations—manifests itself in relations among the middle and upper classes in America, where there is a constant attempt to avert the incipient violence in human relations by means of perpetual institutionalized mutual stroking: people are extraordinarily *nice* to one another. As Garcin puts it, when the protagonists have recognized the antagonisms built in to their situation, "we shall have to be extremely polite to each other" (NE 9). Sartre was savagely critical of this phenomenon in his depiction of Gomez's arrival in the United States in the opening pages of the final volume of *Roads to Freedom*. To the foreigner first arriving in the United States, American politeness is initially a relief—especially if one is used to the relative truculence, rudeness, and general bloody-mindedness of the French—until one realizes that this niceness is largely superficial and meaningless If people were *really* to talk to one another—that is to say, be present and naked to one another in the true form of their relations to one another (ruthless competition for a piece of the cake)—they would soon be at one another's throats. Sartre has depicted the logical conclusion to this state of affairs in *No Exit*. At one point the infernal trio try to put an end to their collective torment of one another by agreeing to stop interacting altogether and remaining silent.

This intense secret anxiety about the real nature of social relations in the United States is perfectly justified: to shout an obscenity out of the window of one's car at an inconsiderate driver anywhere in Europe is not, generally speaking, to take your life in your hands, as it most certainly is here. And it is almost exclusively in the United States (although this is starting to change—witness the recent case in Thatcher's Britain) that you find the perennial madman—driven berserk by his inability to "have a nice day" and participate in the American dream—who marches into a fast-food restaurant and proceeds to try and massacre as many people as possible before he is eventually swatted by the police. (It should be mentioned that these individuals are almost always white males—those members of the population who are most powerfully persuaded (because of racial and sexual discrimination) that they have an inalienable *right* to the dream, and therefore react most violently, feel most directly threatened by the possiblity of being labeled failures, when they have not achieved the dream.) The stronger tradition of neo-socialist welfare programs in Europe and a stronger tradition of an anticapitalist ethos (both the fruits of decades of working-class struggle), have made the frequency of such incidents in the otherwise no less capitalist Western Europe much lower. However, the impulse is clearly a possibility in Europe. Sartre himself wrote a short story, "Erostrate," describing exactly such an individual and such an incident—a text for which my American students, significantly it seems to me, demonstrate a curious enthusiasm, and which they regularly prefer to all of Sartre's other texts.

Dirty Hands: the Supercession of "Bourgeois Moralism" by a Socialist Ethic

This play is set during the Second World War in a fictitious East European country called Illyria, whose circumstances resemble at a number of points the real historical situations which prevailed in several countries at the time. The ruling monarchy had allied the country with Nazi Germany and declared war against the Soviet Union. The second major political force in the country at the outset of the play is a party of bourgeois nationalist liberals (called the Pentagon) which had gone underground and fought the Germans, the fascist monarchy, as well as the third and least power-

198

ful force in the country—the local communist party, which was equally clandestine, equally opposed to both the monarchy and the Germans, and to which the protagonists of the play all belong.

The action of the play is precipitated by a disagreement in the communist party leadership over policy. As the tide of war on the Eastern Front has turned against Germany after its defeat at the hands of the Russians at Stalingrad, its former allies and even some of its opponents are running for cover. The monarchy and the Pentagon both understand that a German defeat will entail occupation by a victorious Soviet army which will give them short shrift. They realize that the only party in Illyria to have retained the Soviets' confidence is the local communist party. They therefore agree to bury their own differences and put out feelers in order to try and entice the communists into negotiations to set up a government of national unity which they will dominate, and which will not be toppled by the invading Soviets because of communist support and participation. One faction of the communist party leadership, represented in the play by a dogmatic hardliner called Louis, argues that such negotiations would constitute an unacceptable compromise with the moral principles which the proletarian party has stood for in its historic struggle with the land-owning aristocracy (represented by the fascist dictatorship of the monarchy) and the urban bourgeoisie (represented by the Pentagon party). Any negotiations with the historic class enemies would constitute class treason. Another faction of the party leadership, represented by one Hoederer, realizes that this transparently opportunistic move on the part of their national enemies presents a golden opportunity: the communist party is too small to impose itself alone; it could only come to power with Soviet tanks at its back, in which case it would be perceived by the population as a puppet government installed by a foreign power. Furthermore, it would earn for itself all the unpopularity which would be the consequence of the necessarily tough sacrifices which a policy of postwar reconstruction would entail and which *any* government would have to impose. A communist government in these circumstances would face a constant risk of popular insurrection. On the other hand, the presence of the approaching Soviet armies means that the monarchy and the Pentagon party are negotiating from a position of weakness. They can be forced to accept minority positions in a central committee of a government of national unity while being obliged to assume the ministerial posts from which the unpopular measures of reconstruction dictated by the central committee will be implemented. Within a matter of months the country will be crying for the communists to be given their chance at the head of the country, in ministerial positions as well as the central committee.

Hoederer's policy is adopted, whereupon the minority hard-line faction decides to have him eliminated. Louis's youthful admirer and acolyte, Hugo Barine, who as a young bourgeois intellectual recruit to the party is eager to prove his mettle and establish that he is not only good for reading books, is presented to Hoederer as his new secretary, with a secret mission to assassinate him. Hugo and his even younger wife, Jessica, join Hoederer at the villa from which he is directing party operations (surrounded by bodyguards, for he has anticipated a possible assassination attempt against him) while awaiting the negotiators from the palace and the Pentagon. Hoederer is clearly Sartre's positive pole of reference in the play, deliberately counterpoised for aesthetic purposes to the youthfully naïve, idealistic, self-hating Hugo. He is clearly a born leader. Unlike Hugo he is a man who knows exactly what he is doing and why, highly intelligent, strong-willed, ruthless when necessary and yet compassionate and big-hearted, and knowing how to inspire enduring love in those who surround him. Whereas Hugo is in the party primarily to escape his family and in order to defy and wound his father—a motive he rationalizes by means of a rhetoric of political idealism—Hoederer is in the party because he loves his fellow human beings unconditionally and sees the communist party as the best means available for improving their lot and his own.

Both Hugo and Jessica swiftly fall under the spell of Hoederer, and the dramatic tension of the play is generated by the conflict Hugo experiences between the duty he feels he has to fulfill his mission and the growing love he feels for his intended victim, who he gradually realizes is not only right where Louis was wrong, but is also the viable father figure he had never had and who is more than willing to help him toward a successful accession to adulthood and maturity. Furthermore, Hoederer swiftly realizes Hugo's secret designs on his life as well as the conflict he is experiencing, and does his best—at no small risk to his own life—to help Hugo renounce the assassination attempt without being humiliated by what he inevitably con-

siders his failure "to be a man." Under the strain of
the taxing circumstances in which they find themselves, and because their relationship was not an adult
one anyway, Jessica and Hugo's marriage crumbles—a
fact neither has any difficulty in accepting, as both of
them have come to love Hoederer, who is the first really powerful and authentic attachment of their lives.
Hoederer reveals his knowledge of the assassination
plot to Hugo and offers him his help and friendship in
overcoming his personal conflicts. At which point Jessica, unbeknownst to Hugo, offers herself unconditionally to Hoederer. Hugo surprises them in an embrace
and, giving way to the worst impulses, is able to screw
up the courage to shoot Hoederer.

After spending two years in prison he is released.
The faction of the party led by Louis now wants him
liquidated, however, as shortly after Hoederer's assassination the Soviet Union had directed the local communist party to adopt precisely the policy Hoederer
had advocated. Thus Hugo is now a potential embar-
rassment to the party if he announces that he killed
Hoederer for any reason other than marital jealousy.
He is given the chance to explain his motives in order
that he may be judged "recuperable" for continued service to the party. He realizes clearly what is at stake
and that his reason for killing Hoederer was certainly
not the difference of political opinion, which was originally supposed to have been the correct motive for
shooting him. He effectively commits suicide, however,
by defiantly declaring that he had killed Hoederer for
political reasons—refusing thereby to accept the new
party line—and is summarily executed. He does this
partly out of loyalty to Hoederer, who he feels deserved

to die for a cause rather than in a fight over a woman, and more fundamentally because he is still heartbroken at Hoederer's death, and knows that killing the first person he had ever truly loved was the worst mistake in a life littered with blunders.

The central theme of the play is a constant interrogation of political morality. Should one compromise with one's political principles in order to achieve one's political objectives? Is it acceptable, as a political leader, to lie to one's supporters if this is necessary to bring them round to accepting a policy which is in their best interests? Is assassination a legitimate instrument of policy? Some of the play's most interesting and thoughtful moments arise in the course of impassioned arguments between Hugo and Hoederer, as the former tries to invalidate the latter's positions in order to be able to persuade himself to go ahead with the assassination. Hugo consistently presents his opposition to the imminent deal with the fascists and nationalist bourgeoisie as a *principled* objection: thus the party should only take power in the course of violent struggle, rather than as the result of a *marchandage* (financial haggling), refusing to compromise with its enemies in order to retain its ideological purity. When Hoederer points out that a deal with the monarchy means that maybe as many as a hundred thousand lives may be spared, Hugo replies that one does not conduct revolutions "with flowers." At which point Hoederer is able to reply:

Hoederer: You see! You don't like people, Hugo. You only like principles. . . .
Hugo: I joined the party because its cause is just and

I will leave it when its cause is no longer so. As for people, I'm not interested in what they are but what they can become.

Hoederer: And I, I love them for what they are. With all their filth and all their vices.... For me it makes a difference that there is one more or one less person in the world. That's precious. I know you well, kid, you are a destroyer. You hate people because you hate yourself; your purity of principles resembles death and the revolution you dream of is not ours: you don't want to change the world, you want to blow it to pieces (DH 225).

It is important to understand that Sartre is not writing merely against a naïve and bloodthirsty idealism in communist politics. Above all he is writing against what, as a Marxist, he calls "bourgeois moralism." Hugo is a young intellectual from the *haute bourgeoisie* who—like many young bourgeois intellectuals — has joined the party out of political idealism and, above all, in order to rebel against his family and find a solution to the personal conflicts his upbringing has engendered in him. (For example, what really bugs him about the proposed deal with the parties opposed to the communists is the fact that it appears to recognize his father, and the social class he represents, as viable interlocutors rather than people simply to be wiped out.) He seeks, in other words, to find the kind of moral order in the communist party which was talked about in the milieu in which he grew up (the kind of rhetoric about freedom, justice, and truth which politicians everywhere are always mouthing) but which was constantly betrayed in practice. Thus, challenging Hoederer for lying to the party militants, he declares that everyone in his family lied and that it is only since he has joined the party that he breathes freely. Hoederer immediately dispels this illusion about the communist party: "But we've always told a few lies" (DH 223). Hugo's stake in the party, in other words, bears little resemblance to that of the average proletarian members, who are in the party in order to liberate themselves from economic oppression and who are therefore ready to adopt whatever policies will realistically bring these goals closer to realization. He cannot accept, for example, that deals of the kind that Hoederer is proposing might be necessary in order to achieve important practical ends, and that as a consequence purity of principles might not be what is really at stake or even important. Indeed, Hugo's insistence on abstract moral principles—rather than the practical and material consequences of actions for the lives of flesh-and-blood people—is precisely what betrays his continuing dependence upon his own social class: it is an insistence on principles of this kind that characterizes "bourgeois moralism."

It is necessary here to explain Sartre's point of view. Let us take, for example, the sacrosanct principle of bourgeois ideology that every individual be free to pursue happiness. This *sounds* fine; but our societies are *not* just or genuinely egalitarian. For example, a capitalist society does not evince massive disparities of wealth and opportunity just because we have not yet perfected the system to the point where these imperfections will melt away, but because capitalism cannot function *without* inequality. Without a working-class that does not own its means of production and which is thereby forced to sell its labor in order to survive—

and thereby produces profit for those who *do* own the factories, the means of production—*capitalism could not continue to exist.* Of course, the rare individual can "raise himself by his bootstraps" and become a millionaire; some individuals do achieve this and, *in principle, anyone* can do this. Anyone—but not *everyone.* For the simple and obvious reason that not everyone can become the owner of General Motors because who would then work on the assembly line. Just as everyone can in principle win the lottery—but if they did in practice they would get back the same miserable amount they paid for their ticket. What this means is that all those wonderful principles which we mouth like magical incantations—honesty, freedom, equality—while they are not totally meaningless, and would stand for something magnificent in the kind of society where they might have universal significance rather than class-bound meanings—are delusory and dangerously mystifying mumbo jumbo which contribute to political oppression. Thus, the principles of equality of opportunity and free enterprise, for example, clearly do not mean the same thing in the case of welfare recipients or major corporations: the former are considered objects of grudging charity and reprehensibly lazy, while the latter are rarely represented in these terms when they are either directly bailed out of financial trouble by the federal government or given large tax breaks at the expense of the working-class tax payers. (Doubtless, measures of this kind provide the latter with work; and it is doubtless preferable to have work in a society where the alternative is unemployment; but they simultaneously provide the owners with something far better: leisure, vast and disproportionate material comfort, expensive educations for their children, among so many other things. And these things are bought with the work of the working classes.)

For Sartre it is precisely because, in a society based on social classes, the moral exigences of pure ethical principles cannot be genuinely fulfilled that their invocation as the sole yardstick whereby political action is judged becomes a means to inhibit action that might entail real material social change. Thus, in answer to the Hoederers of this world, one regularly hears the following objection: How can you claim to be trying to establish peace and justice on earth when you are having recourse to murder? It's a contradiction in terms! In other words, the requirement that one's political actions always be rigorously consistent with certain fixed and rigid moral principles (nonviolence, truthfulness, direct democracy) is made *in order not to have to address the fundamentally contradictory and immoral nature of actual social existence and, above all, in order not to have to change it.* For it is not possible to act effectively for political change in many situations, in our societies as they are presently constituted, without transgressing every moral principle under the sun. To insist on strict adherence to moral principles in these circumstances, therefore, is effectively to advocate inaction, which for Sartre, is not the neutral abstention from the messy arena it likes to represent itself as being, but a tacit endorsement of the status quo. This does not mean that, for a Marxist like Hoederer or Sartre, violence is always to be espoused in a doctrinaire fashion. For example, the nonviolent tactics of Gandhi's resistance to the British Empire in India were clearly suitable and efficacious means to adopt in a situation where the stakes for the British were not sufficiently high and where the British no longer had either the political will or the material means to crush the movement for Indian independence by brute force. On the other hand, in contemporary South Africa, where peaceful resistance to racial discrimination has been drowned in blood, and the government clearly possessed until recently both the will and the means to kill as many people as was necessary to maintain the privileges of a tiny white minority, protracted revolutionary violence, or its imminent possibility, has been, and will continue to be, the most effective means of change. Recent developments—the release of Mandela, moves toward a negotiated settlement, etc.—notwithstanding, it has been the sustained insurrection in the black townships since 1984 that has scared off foreign capital and led to the imposition of sanctions. Violence and its possible escalation are what have brought De Klerk to the negotiating table.

It is necessary to spell all of this out in some detail because we in the United States or Western Europe have a self-serving tendency to get squeamish about violence when it suits us. We conveniently forget, for example, that George Washington clearly shared Sartre's, Lenin's or Mandela's views on this question.

It is the mindless appeal to high-minded principles which cannot be realized given the present social arrangements that leads to their being merely mouthed—that is to say, invoked in theory (not infrequently with the best of intentions by individuals who are genuinely troubled by social injustices), only to be ignored in practice. This is the reason for the constant schizophrenic rift which exists between official discourse and unofficial practice in public and private affairs (rather than individual turpitude). For the Marxist Hoederer, therefore, it is necessary to assume the contradictory and immoral reality of actual social existence and recognize that, on occasion, one can only fight it with its own instruments: violence, lies, hatred, and terror.

It is for all of these reasons that Hoederer is so bewildering to the young Hugo and to the bourgeois moralists that, in Sartre's view, our societies take great care to ensure that we all are. Thus, Hoederer has no difficulty with, on the one hand, lying to the grass-roots communist militants if that is what is necessary to push through a policy which is in the long-term interests of the party, and, on the other hand, in an act of love, knowingly risking his own life (by turning his back to Hugo who is hesitating on the verge of gunning him down) in order to make a moral and emotional point to Hugo: namely, that there is an emotional bond between the two men and that Hoederer has faith in Hugo as a human being—an assurance that the latter, as an insecure and confused young man desperate to prove himself, urgently needs, as Hoederer well knows. It is for the same reasons that Hoederer feels no personal animosity toward either Hugo or Louis for having recourse to his assassination: in their shoes he would do the same. What, after all, could be more normal in political life in societies riven by murderous political conflict and oppression? If one can, for example, introduce economic policies which increase the likelihood of there existing, or continuing to exist, a differential between life-expectancy rates in different groups (for example, blacks and whites in the United

States), then why should one balk at the violent elimination of one's opponents if that is what it takes to put an end to such a state of affairs? (Sartre, however, opposed terrorism in bourgeois democracies because it was counterproductive.) It is for reasons like these that Hoederer feels he can point without shame to the fact that he has dirtied his hands, that he has "blood and shit" "up to his elbows." Failure to accept the necessity of these kinds of compromises with "principles" is simply to look for a pretext for doing nothing—to be, in short, a moral coward. As he puts it to Hugo:

> How afraid you are to dirty your hands. Well, stay pure! What purpose will that serve, and why have you joined us? Purity is a notion for fakirs and monks. You other people, the intellectuals, the bourgeois anarchists, you use it as a pretext for doing nothing. Doing nothing, remaining immobile, pressing your elbows in against your bodies, wearing gloves. For my part, I have dirty hands. Up to the elbows. I have plunged them in shit and in blood. So what? Do you think one can govern innocently? (DH 223–24)

Which is why Hoederer has no problem with forming a government with his worst enemies (as long as, of course, his cause ultimately prevails over theirs). What is at stake for Hoederer is not principles, but practical political efficacy. But, as should be abundantly obvious by now, this is in no way to be confused with the amoral, ruthless cynicism of a moral nihilist or psychopath.

Indeed, significantly, Hoederer inspires love and deep respect in those who surround him. Both Hugo and Jessica fall under his spell, and, interestingly, his charm is described as a function of his appearing "real" to both of them. This is a function of the fact that, unlike both Hugo and Jessica, Hoederer is that rare individual who incarnates Sartre's ideal of existential freedom—that is, someone who has chosen his objectives and projects in good faith. Unlike Hugo—who has chosen the communist party for reasons other than those he proclaims (he is much more interested in defying his father than in liberating the proletariat), and who for this very reason is not truly free because he has made this choice in order to impress someone else (albeit unfavorably) rather than because he, in his freedom of choice, wants it for what it is—unlike Hugo, Hoederer knows what he is doing. He has taken the full measure of the tasks at hand and accepts unflinchingly their cruel exigencies and iron imperatives. The fact that Hugo quite literally does not know what he is doing determines his every act in the play and eventually leads to his death. Thus, it is because he is still a child—someone who has not become his own source of authority, the sole ultimate arbiter of his own decisions—that he is fatally drawn to the dogmatic and doctrinaire Louis, who, he says, "cannot be wrong" (DH 226). Similarly he volunteers for the mission to assassinate Hoederer—not because he is genuinely outraged by Hoederer's policy and because, as the result of a hardheaded assessment, he perceives the mortal danger it represents to the party (he is merely following Louis's line) but because he wishes to convince others and, above all, himself that he really is the tough, adult, militant (like Hoederer) which he is not. Which is why, when he does eventually shoot Hoederer, it is against his best impulses and in his worst possible interests (he loves this man, and feels happier in his presence than he has ever felt in his life). He finally screws up the courage (if one can call it that) to shoot Hoederer when he discovers Jessica in Hoederer's arms, at a point in the play when he and his wife have freely acknowledged to each other the failure of their marriage. Furthermore, he is not even jealous of Jessica's marital infidelity so much as he is angered by an erroneous belief that Hoederer has offered him his help in order to get his hands on Jessica. (A belief one cannot help but feel is self-serving—fastened upon in order to enable him to be angry enough to kill Hoederer and thereby earn what he thinks of as adulthood the quick and easy way.) In short, he is not even able to kill Hoederer for what might, in his world, pass for the right reasons—political reasons—but has to transform his act into a *crime passionel,* the founding act of the bourgeois drawing room drama par excellence. In a final reductio ad absurdum of his existence, at the end of the play, when he has been interrogated as to his motives for the shooting, he is still trying to square the circle of his life by turning his real motives (a need to prove himself as a tough guy, jealousy)—the worst motives he could have had (infantile, ungenerous, and ignoble) but the right ones as far as the party is concerned, given the new line—into the "right" motives so that he can somehow make his peace with Hoederer and atone for having killed him. Such a spectacular failure of a life, such a constant lack of accord between desire and performance, between objectives and outcome, between real and declared motives—in short, such a failure of freedom—can only end in untimely death.

To return briefly to one of the reasons for Hugo's attraction to Hoederer—the fact that Hoederer seems "real"—it should be recalled that at the outset of the play Hugo complains of having the feeling of being permanently in a dream. Revisiting a room that had been familiar to him before going to prison, he tells its owner:

> I wasn't mistaken about your room. Not once. It's all just as I remembered it. Simply, when I was in prison, I would say to myself: "It's a memory. The real room is over there, on the other side of the wall." I have gone in, I've looked at your room, and it did not seem more real than my recollection. The cell as well, it was a dream. And Hoederer's eyes, the day I shot him. Do you think I have a chance of waking up? (DH 140–41)

We are now in a position to understand this sensation: if, as we have just seen, Hugo is never in accord with himself, then he can never be fully present to the world (and vice versa). If, in other words, like Hugo one is engaged in militant political activity for reasons other than the objectives posited and set by that political activity (without really acknowledging these other reasons, yet nonetheless remaining uneasily aware of them), then inevitably the *reality* of that activity will be subtly diminished in one's eyes. One will have this constant nagging suspicion that one is merely going through the motions—that one is, in short, in a dream.

Both Hugo and Jessica complain of this sense of diminished reality, and both of them only feel themselves to be really alive in the presence of Hoederer. In both cases the play establishes a link between their unreality and their youthfulness and unresolved attachments to their families. Hugo is constantly afraid that he will end up resembling his father and therefore, in the classic Freudian pattern generated by the nuclear family, spends his time in phantasmatic ritual slayings of the father by rebelling against him. Indeed, his father had told him, "I too, when I was your age, belonged to a revolutionary group; I wrote in their newspaper. You'll get over it just as I did" (DH 146). There is a sense, therefore, in which Hugo's need for extreme action—his volunteering for the assassination—is presented to us as arising from a desire to commit himself to revolutionary politics by means of an irreparable act of such gravity that any chance of his resembling his father by returning to his class of origin will be foreclosed. This explanation seems all the more compelling to the extent that Hoederer, as a figure of power and authority in the new organization to which Hugo now belongs, inevitably represents to Hugo, as an object of phantasmatic fulfillment, a father figure who can now be slain in the flesh. And, of course, Hugo does indeed "transfer," as Freud put it, his filial sentiments to Hoederer—with the disastrous consequences we have seen.

The fact that at the age of twenty-one, as a married man, Hugo "does not want to live" (DH 146) as he puts it, and that he has these unreduced neurotic family attachments and a pathetic need to be trusted ("And you will *really* have confidence in me?" DH 148)—all of this suggests that one dimension of this play is a reiteration of Sartre's hostility to the nuclear family we have already detected in his other works. The implication seems to be that youth, in the special form it takes

in the bourgeois nuclear family, is an unhealthy pro-
longation of infantilism: the crushing presence of a terrifying castrating father seems to condemn the male
child (we will examine Jessica's case shortly) to childishness, an inability to assume autonomy: hence
Hugo's authoritarianism—his need to subordinate his
own freedom and autonomy of thought to the views of
the dogmatic Louis, the need he expresses for "discipline" (DH 177). Furthermore, it will be what Freud
called castration-anxiety—the refusal, on the part of
men, of passivity or subordination to other men[8] (the
last-minute rejection of the proferred paternal hand of
Hoederer in favor of the violent overthrow of the father)—that is to say, mainstream macho competitiveness among males, which will doom Hugo.

Sartre passes a similar judgment on the condition of
female children with Jessica's questions:

> Why has no one taught me anything? ... I've been
> installed in your men's world now for nineteen
> years, strictly forbidden to touch the objects on dis-
> play, and you made me believe that everything was
> going allright and that I had nothing to do except
> put flowers in vases.... Why have you all left me in
> ignorance, if it was to confess to me one day that this
> world is falling apart all over the place and that
> you're a bunch of incompetents? (DH 215)

The consequences of the enforced infantilization which
is the female's lot in the classic bourgeois nuclear family—her being reduced to a helpless decorative object—
combined with Hugo's own unreality or childishness,
condemn Jessica to a sexual frigidity which is alluded
to at several points in the play. This is simply the

result of the fact that neither she nor her husband are real, or complete, people, in the sense that they have not taken their lives in hand and are thereby incomplete agents. On the terms that the play establishes for itself, love cannot exist between half-people or adolescents. Jessica and Hugo have effectively been playing at love, at marriage, at life itself—a point that is constantly made during their interaction on stage, but most graphically in the simultaneously charming and sinister moment immediately after the fruitless search of their room by Hoederer's bodyguards when they wrestle on their bed for possession of Hugo's revolver, convulsed with laughter, with Jessica shouting "Careful! the gun's going to go off!" (DH 182). As in the case of Hugo, Jessica, like many daughters of nuclear families, is still in the thrall of her father and, like Hugo, falls for Hoederer because he represents an ideal father (she mentions three times that his office reminds her of her father) onto whom she can make a positive transference and with whom she can thereby work through her unreduced conflicts in order to attain authentic adulthood.

That Hugo should have chosen to come through the door to find Hoederer and Jessica at just the wrong moment, with such fatal consequences for all concerned, powerfully conveys Sartre's sense that no chance occurrence can be favorable to anyone once such dangerous and explosive psychic cocktails have been concocted by systematically pathogenic social structures. *Dirty Hands* is one of the most tragic of Sartre's works. The sense of utter defeat, waste, and loss for all the characters by the end of the play (Hugo in particular) is frightful. A more optimistic outcome to essentially the same problematic will be formulated in Sartre's next major play, *The Devil and the Good Lord.*

Before we leave *Dirty Hands,* however, one last remark should be made. At the time of the play's first performances it was widely received as being an anticommunist statement. Hugo's tragedy was seen as the product of an immoral opportunism of the communist leaders in Moscow who see fit to change policy and rewrite history (standard Stalinist practice) whenever short-term political objectives suit their doing so. Hugo was seen as dying for the principle of truth—refusing to accept a mendacious interpretation of Hoederer's assassination. This interpretation of the play prevailed to the extent that the French right-wing press praised it to the skies and the French Communist Party felt obliged to denounce Sartre in the most virulent terms.

This interpretation of the play as anticommunist was far from Sartre's intentions, and he felt obliged for many years to forbid the play's performance anywhere in the world unless it was first endorsed by the local communist party. Our own reading of the play should indicate the extent to which an anticommunist reading of it is erroneous: as we have seen, Sartre's postbourgeois ethic has no problem with about-turns in party policy if the political situation requires them. Furthermore, if we can imagine for a moment Hoederer's being able, from beyond the grave, to advise Hugo in the dilemma he faces at the end of the play—whether or not to be "recuperable," whether or not to accept the false version of Hoederer's death—one has to conclude that Hoederer would have advised Hugo to go along with the party line and continue to make himself useful rather than throw his life away. Hoederer himself, after all, had initiated the false version of his assassination—telling his bodyguards in his dying moments that he was sleeping with Jessica—in order to spare Hugo's life and in order to preserve party unity. In other words, the only extent to which Hugo can attempt to mitigate, if not to redeem, the tragic blunder of killing the only person he has ever loved is not to throw his own life away in a grand, but perfectly futile, gesture, but to continue the work of the man he loves and to which he is supposed to be committed. But to do this would require not only a more authentic political commitment than Hugo really has; it would also require a greater personal strength and willingness to continue to face and assume the tragic consequences of his blunder than he is really capable of. Above all, it would take a degree of modesty—a willingness to engage with the necessary imperfection and general messiness of real political activity—which his bourgeois idealism and youthful extremism are unable and unwilling to come to terms with. Far from constituting an authentic indictment of Stalinist rewritings of history, his suicide is effectively an abdication from any attempt to make a success of his life and the cause he is, in principle, committed to.

The Devil and the Good Lord: the Legitimation of Violence and Revolutionary Terror

This play is in many respects a continuation of the exploration of the problematic of political morality undertaken in *Dirty Hands*. It is set in the sixteenth-century Germany of the Lutheran Reformation; Sartre's most important source for his play seems to have been Engels's book on the Peasant War of 1524–25. Engels interpreted the Protestant Reformation as a first attempt to overthrow the feudal aristocracy and accede to the modern bourgeois world; and in the figure of Thomas Munzer, the Anabaptist leader of the peasants' revolt, who had preached a kind of evangelical communism, Engels saw one of the first modern revolutionary socialists. The proletarian and peasant militants in the play, Nasti and Karl, who present themselves simultaneously as social revolutionaries and "prophets," and in whose discourse millenarian socialism and divine revelation are inextricable, are at once reminiscent of the utopian vision of Munzer and an age in which political thought had to express itself in religious garb because this was the only instrument available. Sartre would mention, in interviews on the subject of the play,[9] how much he had been impressed, in his historical research of the period, by the extent to which religious conflicts in the sixteenth century were unfailingly expressions of class conflicts. This is an important dimension of the play which should be borne in mind if one is not otherwise to find the religious setting disconcerting or bewildering: as we shall see, it is a constant concern of the play to demonstrate that the religious positions or choices of the protagonists are always also political or socioeconomic ones.

This is especially important for an understanding of the metaphysical/political evolution of the main character, Goetz, who, for the first third of the play, is self-consciously and deliberately committed to pure evil—a commitment he is singularly well-placed to fulfill as Germany's foremost general. This choice is presented as an attempt to find an existential solution to the fact that he is the illegitimate son of a noble mother and a peasant father. A walking social contradiction, profoundly humiliated by the stigma attached to this condition, he has sought to escape his shame by launching an all-out attack on the ultimate guarantor and architect of the moral and social order which oppresses him—in his feudal, religious, age, God himself. This project is conceived in terms the grandiloquence and *hauteur* of which betray its origins in humiliated pride:

> *Goetz*: You needn't worry; I shall take it [the city of Worms].
> *Catherine*: But why?
> *Goetz*: Because it is wrong.
> *Catherine*: Why should you want to do wrong?
> *Goetz*: Because Good has already been done.
> *Catherine*: By whom?
> *Goetz*: By God the Father. Me, I invent (DGL 46).

He likes to think that his commitment to evil—the betrayal of his brother Conrad, his projected destruction of Worms, his humiliation of all around him—constitutes a serious threat to the established political and social order. The proletarian militant Nasti, who expresses Sartre's opinion at this point, seeks to dispel Goetz's illusions in this respect:

> You bring about disorder. And disorder is the best servant of established power. You weakened the entire order of chivalry the day you betrayed Conrad, and you'll be weakening the bourgeoisie the day you

destroy Worms. Who will profit by your action? The rulers. You serve the rulers, Goetz, and you will serve them whatever you do; all destruction brings confusion; weakens the weak, enriches the rich, increases the power of the powerful (DGL 53).

Nasti proposes to Goetz that he join their social revolution, to which the latter responds with a question as to what his place would be in the new political order. Nasty replies, "The equal of everyone else" (DGL 54). Like many of those who have been discriminated against and humiliated, Goetz has overcompensated with insane pride; and so the notion of a vulgar equality with his fellow human beings is repugnant to him at this stage in the play. He turns down Nasti's proposal because he believes that God alone can be a worthy adversary for him:

> *Nasti*: Then you will go on being nothing but a useless uproar?
> *Goetz*: Useless, yes. Useless to men. But what do I care for mankind? God hears me, it is God I am deafening, and that is enough for me, for he is the only enemy worthy of me.... It is God I shall crucify this night, through you, and through twenty thousand men, because his suffering is infinite.... This city will go up in flames. God knows that. At this moment, he is afraid, I can feel it.... The city shall blaze; the soul of the Lord is a hall of mirrors, the fire will be reflected in a thousand mirrors. Then I shall know that I am an unalloyed monster (DGL 55).

At this point Goetz's commitment to evil is challenged by the priest Heinrich. Heinrich himself has had to deal with a contradiction that is impossible for

221

him to negotiate: as a Catholic priest his first allegiance is to the Church; however, he has taken his ministry of his parish—constituted for the most part by the poor—very seriously. Because of the political situation of the Church at the time—squarely on the side of the political and economic establishment—Heinrich will be subjected to an insurmountable conflict of loyalties when civil strife breaks out. Forced to choose between allowing two hundred priests to be slaughtered by an insurrectional mob in Worms and supplying the Church's ally, Goetz, with the means to enter Worms, save the priests, and massacre the starving mobs of poor people, he eventually betrays his parishioners. Horrified by what he has done—and above all by the fact that he *had* to be a traitor to one or other of the two parties involved—Heinrich loses his mind and succumbs to a paranoid delusion to the effect that he is permanently accompanied by the Devil. Impressed by the ineluctability of the evil of his own acts, he formulates the following ethic, challenging Goetz's belief that evil is his own personal choice:

> You are giving yourself a lot of trouble for nothing, you braggart of vice. If you want to deserve hellfire, you need only remain in your bed. The world is iniquity; if you accept it, you are an accomplice; if you should try to change it, then you become an executioner (DGL 63).

(Here Sartre is presenting what, in his opinion, is the standard pessimistic bourgeois response to a call to arms in the cause of political justice: political revolution inevitably culminates in the likes of Stalin and Pol Pot. This view conveniently forgets that our Western democracies could only come into existence as a consequence of the kinds of bloody struggles exemplified by the French, American, and English Revolutions.) This is a challenge to Goetz, of course, who likes to think that he is the sole author of his acts. If evil is inevitable, then his deliberate defiance of God is pointless. Therefore, he has to rise to Heinrich's challenge, and declares that good is not only possible but that he, Goetz, will become a saint by a mere act of will. Both men agree to judge the success or failure of Goetz's project a year and one day later.

Goetz's saintly phase turns out to be if anything even more disastrous for those around him than his demonic one, a fact which is designed, of course, to serve Sartre's didactic intention. His first act is to repudiate Catherine, the young woman he had forced, in yet another act of willed evil, to be his concubine. Goetz's sheer force of character and his intelligence had ended up seducing Catherine, however, and she had fallen in love with him. His repudiation of her in the name of Christian morality breaks her heart, makes her feel dirty and sinful, and eventually kills her. Goetz next proceeds to distribute his lands and possessions to the peasants bound to his lands, and founds there a utopian community where Christian love is obligatory and all strife forbidden. The outcome is catastrophic. First, these measures, as acts of charity, humiliate and dehumanize the peasants even more than their previous feudal bondage, which was at least frankly and openly oppressive. Second, the redistribution of land by Goetz places the entire landowning class in Germany under pressure to do likewise. A fresh peasant revolt breaks out; the utopian commu-

nity is burned to the ground, its inhabitants are massacred by the peasant insurgency because they will not
espouse revolutionary violence, and by the end of the
play the peasant army has already suffered one major
defeat in the field. Goetz tries to handle the catastrophe by retreating into a masochistic and misanthropic
religious ascetism, in which human imperfection will
be chastised in the mortification of his own flesh in the
course of various ordeals he imposes on himself—
thirst, self-flagellation, and so on. He tries thereby to
avoid the whole issue of good and evil in human affairs
by negating the entire human dimension and subordi-
nating it to God. Thus, for example, he refuses to give
way to the love he feels for Hilda, the young peasant
woman who is the sole survivor of the community and
who is caring for him, and does everything to persuade
himself that human flesh (above all, that of woman) is
disgusting and sinful. Sartre's point in all of this is
that if one once recognizes the existence of God, then
one demeans humanity. Or, as Hilda puts it to Goetz,
"How painful you find it to be a man" (DGL 132). The
subordination of life to religion, in other words, is a
means to evade the real challenges of being a human
being engaged in dealing with other human beings.
This has been Goetz's problem all along: humiliated
by human beings, he had retreated into a pose of
haughty disdain for humanity, maintaining real relations only with the divine. People became mere pawns
in the deadly game he was playing with God. As he had
said at the moment of his conversion to saintliness,
"It's still the best means of remaining alone" (DGL 64).

At this point Heinrich reappears—it is the date
agreed upon for them to decide whether Goetz has suc-

224

ceeded in performing good—and once again he provokes a crucial decision on the part of Goetz. Heinrich
swiftly uncovers the true motivation of Goetz's saintliness—misanthropy and a secret urge to destroy—and
Goetz himself is by this stage all too ready to concur
in the indictment:

> Monster or saint, I didn't give a damn, I wanted to
> be inhuman. Say it, Heinrich, say I was mad with
> shame, and wanted to amaze Heaven to escape men's
> scorn. Go on! What are you waiting for? Speak! ...
> [*Imitating Heinrich*] You didn't change your ways,
> Goetz, you changed your language. You called your
> hatred of people love, your rage for destruction you
> called generosity.... I, the accused, acknowledge
> myself to be guilty (DGL 139).

In the course of their conversation Heinrich inadvertently leads Goetz to the very conclusion which he has
secretly arrived at himself, but which in an act of bad
faith he resists acknowledging: God does not exist.

Goetz realizes that the nonexistence of God means
that he is free, that only his fellow human beings and
the relations he has with them count for anything. He
is ready to start life all over again and embrace an
ordinary human existence. This conclusion is intolerable to Heinrich, who has a classically Protestant conception of good and evil and its consequences: although
he had recognized the evil of his own actions, and had
concluded that evil was unavoidable, he had always
counted on being redeemed through mere faith. The
death of God means that his sole judges must be other
people—a conclusion which he cannot abide, for he
knows that he will not be exculpated by his own kind

(he has not even been able to forgive himself). He dies attempting to kill Goetz as the hateful exponent of a view that makes his life intolerable.

Goetz now realizes that his salvation lies with other people, that he *needs* other people: he is ready to serve his apprenticeship of modesty. He presents himself to the leadership of the peasant army, asking that he be allowed to serve its cause:

Nasti: Why?
Goetz: I need you. [Pause.] I want to be a man among men.
Nasti: Only that?
Goetz: I know: it's the most difficult of all things. That's why I must begin at the beginning.
Nasti: What is the beginning?
Goetz: Crime. Men of the present day are born criminals. I must demand my share of their crimes if I want to have my share of their love and virtue. I wanted pure love: ridiculous nonsense. To love anyone is to hate the same enemy; therefore I will adopt your hates. I wanted to do Good: foolishness. On this earth at present Good and Evil are inseparable. I agree to be evil in order to become good (DGL 145).

He is persuaded by Nasti to assume the generalship, and his first act—in line with the new realist conception of ethics just formulated above—is to stab to death one of the peasant leaders who challenges his position at the head of the army. This is a deliberate tactical move: the peasant army is demoralized after its recent defeat, desertions are on the rise, the leaders are already talking about throwing in the towel. Goetz realizes he must impose an iron discipline if he is to lead the army to victory:

226

Listen to me! I take up this command against my will, but I shall be relentless. Believe me, if there is one chance of winning this war, I shall win it. Proclaim immediately that any soldier attempting to desert will be hanged. By tonight, I must have a complete list of troops, weapons, and stores; you shall answer for everything with your lives. We shall be sure of victory when your men are more afraid of me than of the enemy ... [*Goetz kicks the body.*] The kingdom of man is beginning. A fine start! (DGL 148–149).

This acceptance of the most ruthless violence—revolutionary terror—as a necessary and inescapable dimension of revolutionary political change marks this play, with *Dirty Hands,* as Sartre's most politically radical, or activist, work. (For the Sartrean rationale and justification of revolutionary violence, the reader is referred to the preceding section on *Dirty Hands*). The play is also, with *Roads to Freeedom,* Sartre's most optimistic work: horrific though they may be, courses of action and practical solutions do exist. This will not be the case for the next play after *The Devil and the Good Lord*—*The Condemned of Altona*—to which we can now turn.

The Condemned of Altona[10]

A. The Death of the Modern Bourgeois Centered Subject

The action of the play takes place during the summer of 1959 when the protagonist, Frantz von Gerlach, is thirty-four. He is the scion of a family which has been Germany's leading shipbuilder during the twentieth century. Frantz's father, who is still at the head of the family enterprise, had been one of the wealthiest and most powerful German capitalists to have compromised with and profited from Hitler's regime. As the eldest son Frantz had been groomed by his father to eventually take over the shipyards and had been ruthlessly molded in his father's image: the elder von Gerlach is a captain of industry in the old style of nineteenth-century entrepreneurs, a prince of the modern bourgeois world—a born leader, lucid, proud, ambitious, strong-willed. Above all, Frantz's upbringing endows him with a powerful sense of responsibility which is compounded by the Protestant cultural tradition which has produced him.

During the war a Polish rabbi escapes from a nearby camp that has been built on land which Frantz's father unscrupulously agreed to sell to the Nazis. Frantz, who is only sixteen at the time, is deeply ashamed of his father's collaboration with the regime and chooses to conceal the escapee in his room in order to redeem the father he loves and admires. Both Franz and his father suspect that they may be denounced by their Nazi chauffeur. In order to retain the initiative, the father telephones Goebbels, Hitler's Minister of Information and Propaganda (who is all too aware of the importance of von Gerlach's shipyards to the Nazi war effort), and gets his son off the hook on condition that he enlist. But of course von Gerlach has had to denounce the rabbi in so doing. The S.S. arrive and the fugitive is murdered before Frantz's eyes while he is himself pinned down by other soldiers. The psychological consequences of the incident prove catastrophic for

Franz: he has been taught that he is a prince who is born to impose his will upon the world, and whose actions *count;* but even the extraordinarily dangerous action of sheltering the rabbi has been nullified by his father's ability to render it harmless for himself and inefficacious for others. He decides that the next time he is in a position to determine the destiny of others he will not allow himself to be reduced to impotence.

Three years later the opportunity to keep this promise arises. He is the commanding officer of a small unit on the Eastern Front whose retreat has been cut off by partisans. Two prisoners may hold the information which could lead to his men's deliverance, and he has to decide their fate. It is intimated to him that there are those among his men who may take matters into their own hands if he is squeamish about having recourse to all the means at his disposal to gain the vital information. In order to forestall his being once again reduced to the position of impotence he dreads, and in order to be the master of the inevitable impending evil at least to the extent of having chosen and assumed it, he decides to torture the prisoners himself:

Four good Germans will pin me to the ground, and my own men will bleed the prisoners to death. No! I shall never again fall into abject powerlessness. I swear it. It's dark. Horror has not yet been unleashed.... I'll keep one move ahead of them. If anyone unleashes it, it will be me. I'll assume the evil; I'll display my power by the singularity of an unforgettable act: I'll change *living* men into vermin. I alone will deal with the prisoners. I'll plunge them into abjection. They'll talk. Power is an abyss and I can see its depths. It is not enough to choose who shall live and who shall die. I shall choose what the reign of the human shall be with a penknife and a cigarette lighter. [*Distractedly*] Fascinating! It is the glory of sovereign subjects to go to Hell. I shall go there (CA 164).

The men die without giving up their secrets, his men are massacred, and Frantz survives, obliged to live knowing that he has committed atrocities *to no avail* because Germany has lost the war. He is tormented by the guilt his Lutheran upbringing induces in him (as a supreme individual or subject he is supremely responsible); his solution to the intolerable situation will be to sequester himself in an upstairs chamber of the family mansion, ministered to only by his sister Leni, refusing to see his father, striving to justify his crimes to himself by cultivating the belief that Germany is being vengefully starved to death by the victorious allies—a horrendous outcome which would amply vindicate his having gone to any lengths to prevent. The truth, of course, is that Germany has already by 1959 risen from the ashes of defeat to become Europe's foremost economic power—a fact which once again (as in the outcome of the incident of the fugitive rabbi) deprives Frantz's actions of both efficacy and meaning. Both the fact that Germany has lost the war and its successful reconstruction transform what he had seen as his willed Luciferian heroism into mere war crimes.

At the end of the play his father explains to him that the United States–Soviet rivalry of the Cold War has led the Americans to ensure that Germany remain in the capitalist camp by giving it preferential treatment on the international markets, and that this is at the origin of the historical irony that the loser of the war has in fact ended up winning it: Germany now has at its disposal those very markets it had originally gone to war over and now enjoys the very hegemony on the continent it had sought in the first place. Furthermore, patriots like Frantz had merely prolonged the slaughter and put eventual reconstruction at risk. His father summarizes his son's career for him by saying that he has done nothing, he is nothing, and there is nothing he can do to redeem his life. The father asks Frantz's forgiveness for having formed him in his own image in order to direct the family company, for von Gerlach now realizes both the catastrophic consequences of this fatal possession by his father for Frantz's life and that the notion of anyone directing the enterprise is a delusion; it is the enterprise itself which calls the tune rather than any human agent:

> My poor boy! I wanted you to run the firm after me. But it does the running. It chooses its own men. It has got rid of me. I own it, but I no longer run it. And you, little prince, it rejected you from the start. What does it need a prince for? It trains and recruits it own managers. . . . I had given you the talents you needed, and my fierce hunger for power, but it was no use. What a pity! In order to act, you took the greatest risks, and, you see, the firm turned all your acts into gestures. In the end, your torment drove you to crime, and because of that very crime it nullifies you. It grows fat on your defeat. I don't like regrets, Frantz. They serve no purpose. If I could believe that you might be useful somewhere else, and in some other capacity. . . . But I made you a

monarch, and today that means: good for nothing (CA 172).

In some respects this is a difficult argument to follow. What is meant is that the capitalist enterprise which the elder von Gerlach has run all his life as if it were his own product has in fact *produced,* and then eliminated, *him:* in order for the company to function efficiently von Gerlach had, in the earlier stages of the existence of the company, to be a certain kind of person: strong-willed, domineering, uncannily shrewd, brilliantly and successfully manipulative of others, ruthlessly lucid, capable of inspiring passionate and abiding affection in those over whom he stands in authority (his three children are bound to him by bonds of steel even in their frequent moments of intense hatred for him—for none of them can abide the idea of his impending death, for example), in short, all the qualities required for an ideal leader of an enterprise of ruthless self-aggrandizement. At a certain moment in time, however, when the sheer size and technological and financial complexity of a vast international corporation is reached, this kind of nineteenth-century entrepreneur becomes obsolete and has to be replaced by technocrats and a managerial personnel who, to fulfill their functions, have to be of quite a different kind of personality. Von Gerlach recognizes this and explains the fact to his younger son, Werner, the family weakling, at the beginning of the play, when the father offers him the directorship of the company:

Werner: To decide! To decide! To be responsible for everything. Alone. On behalf of a hundred thousand men. And you have managed to live!

232

The Father: It's been a long time since I have decided anything. I sign the correspondence. Next year, you will sign it.

Werner: Don't you do anything else?

The Father: Nothing, for nearly ten years.

Werner: Why are you needed? Wouldn't just anyone do?

The Father: Yes, just anyone.

Werner: Me, for example.

The Father: You, for example.

Werner: Nothing is perfect. There are so many cogs in the machine. Suppose one of them were to jam. . . .

The Father: For adjustments, Gelber will be there. A remarkable man, you know, who has been with us for twenty-five years.

Werner: I'm lucky, in fact. He will give the orders.

The Father: Gelber? You're mad! He is your employee. You pay him to let you know what orders to give (CA 11).

It is not for nothing, in other words, that Werner—the weakling, whose only function as director will be to sign the paperwork—rather than the imperious Frantz will be the son who eventually replaces his father at the head of the enterprise. He is just the man for the job. But Sartre's point, in the passage we are still trying to explicate, is stronger than this: not only does the enterprise recruit the kind of men it needs, but it actively intervenes in the historical process in order to reject those who have been intended by other forms of agency (the father, in this instance) to be at its head: "And you, little prince, it rejected you from the start." Frantz's tragedy is to have been born fifty years too late. His father had formed him in his own image because he had believed that what had worked well once would work well a second time round. But in an age of gigantic conglomerates where technocrats and managers exercise the kind of power the new nature of the enterprise requires Frantz is an anachronism and therefore eliminated by the enterprise.

But how can we can we intelligibly speak of an impersonal mass of capital acquiring what sounds suspiciously like quasi-human agency such that it can actively intervene in the lives of people in this fashion?

If we reconsider the murder of the rabbi—the incident which definitively launches Frantz on the path to committing atrocious crimes and ultimate catastrophe—we recall that von Gerlach had originally sold the land on which the concentration camp is built to the Nazi regime because their bellicose policies were in his interests:

> *The Father*: Eighty thousand workers since March. I'm growing. My shipyards spring up overnight. I have the most formidable power.
> *Frantz*: Of course. You work for the Nazis.
> *The Father*: Because they work for me. That bunch: it's the plebs on the throne. But they are at war to find us markets, and I am not going to quarrel with them over a matter of a bit of land (CA 35).

It is the shipyards themselves, in other words, and above all the great mass of capital invested in the shipyards, which demand this policy of cynical compromise in order that they may continue to expand. For like all capitalist enterprises, and indeed like capitalism itself, they can only survive through continued expansion. They have no other raison d'être. Doubtless, von Gerlach was free to reject the Nazis' request for the land, but this would have earned him and his company enemies in high places he could ill afford. To have made a moral stand would have been to repudiate everything his life had stood for up to that point: the endless expansion of his company.

In choosing to compromise with the regime, however, von Gerlach betrays his own fierce individualism: the company is no longer his product, the product of his will which he is free to dash to pieces on a whim. He has, in other words, subordinated, or alienated, his freedom to his own product. His own product now takes priority over his own integrity. The product of his own freedom now calls the shots. This turn of events effectively demystifies the myth of bourgeois individualism—as the unconditioned and superbly untrammeled pure affirmation of personal will—by demonstrating that it was never anything more than capital's instrument anyway. The youthful Frantz for his part, however, still believes in the old myth. He feels that his moral conscience (and his father's, which he wishes to redeem) must affirm itself no matter what the cost. He therefore deliberately invites martyrdom ("Better death than ... "). This is precisely the kind of stand of which Werner would never have been capable, which is why he, and not Frantz, will eventually accede to the directorship of the company. Now, *it is the company which will nullify this suicidal act:* von Gerlach phones Goebbels to save his own skin and that of his son (which is the same thing: "You are me," Frantz says to his father). But von Gerlach *is* the company—he has proved by the sale of his land to the Nazis that he gives priority to the company over the quality of his own life—and furthermore, Goebbels reaches an understanding with von Gerlach because he too understands the crucial importance of von Gerlach for the continued success of the shipyards on which the Nazi war effort depends.

It is the economic imperatives of the shipyards, in other words, which are determining everyone's actions. Except those of Frantz, who is acting contrary to them. But the shipyards get to him anyway through the intermediary of his father and Goebbels, who together render his actions harmless: no one is arrested, there is no scandal, and Frantz is bundled off to the army: "In order to act, you took the greatest risks and, you see, it [the company] transformed all your actions into mere gestures" (CA 172).

Von Gerlach continues: "Your torment finished by driving you to criminal acts and even in crime it [the company] nullified you: it grows fat feeding off your defeat" (CA 172). Germany's (Frantz's) defeat has been the means of the shipyards' ultimate triumph, because of the new realities of the Cold War.

At this point in the play we realize that von Gerlach—who has already indicated, at the beginning of the play, his intention to commit suicide once his affairs are "in order," for he has cancer of the throat—has intended all along to propose to Frantz that they commit joint suicide. He realizes that for both of them there is no other way out. But he has also wanted Frantz to acknowledge that, despite having been condemned to impotence and futility by his father, he alone was reponsible for the decision to have recourse to torture in 1944. Von Gerlach finds his son's evasions of his responsibility, his attempts to justify himself and his age in the course of raving addresses in his room to a tribunal of an imaginary post-Armageddon civilization of crabs of the thirtieth century, to be degrading. It is also, however, von Gerlach's intention to accept his own responsibility in the catastrophe of his son's life and put an end to his son's suffering before his own death puts this beyond his power. Hence the series of revelations at the end of the play in the course of which the father explains to his son his own fatal role in his son's doom. And hence the long and convoluted plot in the course of which von Gerlach has to play Leni against Werner's wife, Johanna, and vice versa, in order to prise Frantz out of his room so that they can speak together one last time.[11] And hence, also, the suicide pact, which Frantz accepts—a finishing touch to the control von Gerlach has exercised over his son's life from start to finish, and which constitutes Sartre's final and most damning of the critical comments on the nuclear family and the relations between parents and their children in such a family structure which litter his plays:

> *Frantz*: Your image will be pulverized together with all those which never left your head. You will have been my cause and my destiny right to the end. . . .
> *The Father*: Very well. . . . I made you. I will unmake you. My death will envelope yours and, in the final analysis, I alone will die (CA 174).

A comparison with *No Exit* is useful at this point. In the earlier play, despite the incorrect English translation of the French title already discussed, there *was* in fact an exit from the protagonists' infernal torment—the door to hell does open at one point and the characters are indeed free to choose freedom over alienation to the Other. Here, however, no way out from sequestration in the hell which is the von Gerlachs' mansion (which serves as a metaphor both for the nuclear family and history itself) exists beyond that of suicide. Both Frantz and his father are irremediably doomed. This conclusion to the later play is a measure of the infinitely more pessimistic assessment of the options open to history's victims (that's all of us—both masters and slaves) at which Sartre has arrived by the late 1950s.

The Condemned of Altona was widely perceived at the time of its first performances—and correctly so—as commenting implicitly on the war for independence which was being fought at the time by the people of Algeria against their French colonial occupiers, a war which in France was as controversial and bitterly divisive of French society as the Vietnam war was in the United States. The French army had committed many atrocities—indiscriminate massacres of civilians and the torture of prisoners—and Sartre himself had played an extremely active part in denouncing them. In interviews Sartre acknowledged that it had been his intention that the play should have this immediately topical resonance. More fundamentally, however, as Sartre also implied in the same interviews (and as the play itself suggests), *The Condemned of Altona* is neither about French colonialism nor about Nazi Germany so much as an attempt rather to create a representative myth of the modern individual of advanced capitalist industrial societies. And in this respect the play is unquestionably the most pessimistic work in Sartre's oeuvre. It is also his most strictly

Marxist literary work. With uncanny rigor it demonstrates the extent to which we have lost mastery of our own product: the enormous tentacular structure of the international capitalist market (and, ultimately, the historical process itself on both sides of the Iron Curtain), in which our collective human activity has accumulated and taken shape as a gigantic swirling process which no one controls and which oppresses everyone—even a family like the von Gerlachs, who are the lords of the earth, great capitalist magnates—choosing and forming our personal identities for us, recruiting those individuals which will best serve it and discarding on the garbage heap of history those whom it has itself rendered obsolete, luring and nudging otherwise decent (exceptional, even, in the case of Frantz) individuals either into direct participation in, or indirect complicity with, wars between the great capitalist powers or, latterly, colonial and neocolonial wars of aggression and domination—the French in Algeria, the Americans in Vietnam, or the Soviets in Hungary and Afghanistan—with their ineluctable attendant criminal atrocities. For by the end of the play Sartre is indicting not just capitalism but an entire species living under the bane of material scarcity—circumstances in which the mere existence of another fellow human being constitutes a threat to my own survival, eliciting a paranoid preemptive first strike:

> Centuries of the future, here is my century, solitary and deformed—the accused. My client is disemboweling himself with his own hands. What you take for white lymph is blood. There are no red corpuscles for the accused is dying of hunger. But I will tell you the

secret of this multiple perforation. The century might have been a good one had not man been watched from time immemorial by the cruel enemy who had sworn to destroy him, that hairless, malignant, carnivorous species, by man. One and one makes one, that's our enigma. The beast was hiding, and suddenly we surprised his look deep in the eyes of our neighbors; so we struck: legitimate self-defense. I took the beast by surprise, I struck, a man fell, in his dying eyes I saw the beast, still living—myself. One and one makes one: what a misunderstanding! (CA 177–78).

The terrifying intellectual and moral rigor of *The Condemned of Altona,* the thoroughness of the demonstration of the fundamental causes of our tragic and desolate condition—a demonstration which never becomes scholastic but always sustains its dramatic force—the play's sombre grandeur, its stench of sulfur and flickering glowering light of universal hellfire ("the horror of being alive," as Johanna puts it at one point in the play), its air of a "twilight of the gods," all this makes *The Condemned of Altona* both Sartre's bleakest and greatest literary work.

B. Why Sartre Is No Longer Fashionable: The Rise of Structuralism and Poststructuralism, and the "Death of the Subject"

Somewhere around thirty years ago Sartre lost the position of extraordinary dominance he had exercised over French intellectual life since the closing days of the Second World War. He was displaced as the primary object of adulation and execration in French letters by a cluster of figures—Lévi-Strauss, Althusser,

Foucault, Lacan, Kristeva, Deleuze, Irigaray, Derrida, and others—none of whom, despite producing much work of importance and considerable worth, have loomed over the intellectual scene quite as Sartre did, but who collectively have elaborated positions which were presented, and have been consistently perceived, as inimical to Sartre and as rendering his philosophical works obsolete. Despite the spuriousness of this view (at least in its strongest formulations) the French public shunted Sartre off to the wings. This was to be Sartre's fate wherever recent French thought has been influential, especially in the United States.

The Condemned of Altona is an especially useful play in terms of which to discuss this development. For the historical reasons for which Frantz von Gerlach is eliminated from history as a kind of industrial waste product, to be replaced by his younger brother Werner, are closely related to the historical changes in the world at large which led to Sartre's fall from grace among French intellectuals and his replacement by structuralists, like Lévi-Strauss, and then poststructuralists, like Derrida. Simplifying considerably, the most important eventual consequence of the work of both these latter groups of writers consisted in the demonstration that the individual subject was a *social construction*. Sartre, of course, knew this too. What else is *The Condemned of Altona* if not such a demonstration? But the terms of the demonstration were quite different in the case of Sartre's successors: again, simplifying and homogenizing the work of this latter group vastly, these writers—in large measure as a consequence of attempting to grapple with a new postindustrial world of information and endless consumerism solicited by a ruthless and interminable reprocessing of the subject's desires through the media—presented this construction of the subject, the very identity of the human subject, as a mere cipher, as it were, in a gigantic cultural system of signs and information burps which embraced, permeated, and formed all existence. The kind of situation where the elder von Gerlach could speak of having personally formed and molded his son in his own image is an impossibility nowadays. People are no longer formed primarily by these intense, incestuously one-on-one, nuclear-familial relationships. (This very fact is the despair of parents as they watch their children being shaped above all by the slime that flows over their living room floors from the television set, the subliminal language spoken by an all-inclusive habitat of consumer objects, the unrelenting barrage of music piped into every corner of the social environment on every pretext, and the well-nigh irresistible pressure of peer groups which serve primarily to relay and consolidate the messages of these influences.)

This new social reality does not lend itself to representation in the older artistic forms like the bourgeois drawing-room theater which is the model for a play like *The Condemned of Altona*. Which is why novels and plays like those of Sartre were abandoned in the 1950s for postmodern experiments like those of Beckett and Ionesco (erroneously described as a "theater of the absurd") and the New Novel (Robbe-Grillet and company), which are distinguished by a self-conscious reflection upon and permanent subversion of literary representation itself which far surpass, say, Sartre's meditations in *Nausea* on the difference between "adventures" and "life" or the ability of words to denote objects. These latter works constitute a response to the construction of the postmodern subject in systems of representation which the investment of the population by sign systems (the media, or consumer objects which collectively form a subliminal language which solicits a very specific desiring subject) has brought into the awareness of artists and the population at large (albeit mostly at a nonthetic, nontheoretical, level). It is within this context that a work like *The Condemned of Altona* appears old-fashioned. Despite the fact that Sartre is acutely aware of the construction of the subject by, ultimately, social forces (the exigencies of an industrial capitalist society in the case of the von Gerlachs), he chooses to depict this construction in an earlier period than our own. His account of that construction is historically and sociologically correct, furthermore; but it does not address *the immediate contemporary concerns of today's* public. Or, if it does, it does so obliquely, by extension or by implication. It is as if Sartre were only able to portray the demise of his own age, without being able to take on its successor.[12] In short, without its greatness being in any way diminished, the play has a faded and dated air to it which makes it a great *classic,* like the dramas of Corneille and Racine. The tone or feel of the play is wrong for contemporary audiences. The two principal characters, Frantz and his father, are titans compared with contemporary subjects; these strong-willed men who only play for the highest stakes are historical dinosaurs, as Sartre well knew. In this respect they resemble Sartre himself, who incarnated the Marxist project to perfection. As the will to transform society in one's own image, as the determination to make men and women the active subjects of their history rather than its helpless objects—in other words, to make history the controlled fulfillment of human intention rather than the opaque impersonal process which crushes us all—the Marxist project is in a sense the apotheosis and accomplishment of the modern individual as it appears to us from the Renaissance down to the Second World War. By contrast, Sartre's successors have been much less ambitious. Derrida, for example, the most redoubtable of these figures, consistently eschews anything that might conceivably look like what has traditionally passed for action or affirmation, and restricts himself to a kind of minimalist tinkering (of a particularly devastating kind) with other people's texts such that they end up collapsing under their own internal contradictions. In this respect his work is an implicit comment on the possibilities for action which are available to the individual in our present circumstances. His work resembles nothing so much as the behavior of an embittered and malevolent petty bureaucrat who, with all possibilities of open revolt foreclosed by the very nature of the social constraints under which he works, nonetheless manages to bring the system crashing down by slyly pushing the wrong papers round in the wrong directions. (To say this is in no sense to indict Derrida personally—different possiblilities are available to different ages.) In this respect he closely resembles Werner von Gerlach—even to the extent of continuing to feel threatened by his elder brother once the latter has definitively disqualified himself from ever occupying the directorship of the company. Long after Sartre had not only faded from the intellectual scene but even died, Derrida was still making snide and resentful remarks about him in interviews. In similar fashion Sartre himself resembled nothing so much as Frantz von Gerlach in his paranoid delusional phases where he is attempting to encapsulate and express the entire history of the twentieth century in order to defend it to a tribunal composed of an imaginary civilization of crabs from the thirtieth century. One thinks of the vast, unprecedentedly ambitious, all unfinished, projects he undertook, such as the *Critique of Dialectical Reason*—which attempted to devise the philosophical instruments which would make it possible, in principle, to unify all human history within one vast narrative—and *The Family Idiot* (three thousand pages long, and only three fifths completed), which attempted to produce a *complete* account of one man's life (Gustave Flaubert) in all its dimensions—historical, sociological, psychoanalytic, and literary.

Long after wrangles for preeminence in Paris have subsided, people will still turn to Sartre to understand the twentieth century. And even if all the lights are blown out, and all that remains in the wasteland of a collapsed planetary ecosystem, or an atomic cinderheap, is a civilization of crabs or cockroaches, Sartre will have nonetheless helped *us, now,* understand our own era. That is an absolute which cannot be destroyed. Each one of his works constituted an attempt to live up to the following admirable conception of literature which he formulated on the final page of *Situations II:* "Through literature, the collectivity switches over into a mode of reflection upon itself, into mediation, it acquires an unhappy or uncomfortable awareness, an image of itself without equilibrium which it ceaselessly seeks to modify and to improve."[13]

That Sartre consistently met this criterion is the basis of our lasting debt to him.

NOTES

1. *Sartre on Theater,* ed. Michel Contat and Michel Rybalka (London: Quartet Books, 1976) 186ff.

2. Quoted in Michel Contat and Michel Rybalka, *Les Ecrits de Sartre* (Paris: Gallimard, 1970) 90; my translation.

3. *The Portable Nietzsche,* trans. Walter Kaufmann and R. J. Hollingdale (New York: Vintage, 1968) 467.

4. See Freud's *Interpretation of Dreams,* ch. 6.

5. In this respect the play anticipates the work of a younger generation of French philosophers, writers like Gilles Deleuze, Luce Irigaray, and Jacques Derrida, who would come to prominence in the late 60s and 70s. Talk of Sartre's challenging patriarchy, however, must be strongly qualified by the absence of any problematization of the fates of Electra and Clytemnestra: for example, would Orestes have felt bound to the same degree to avenge his mother had she been murdered by Agamemnon? etc.

6. There is a risk here, of course, of an anachronistic projection of the forms of the family under bourgeois modernity, and their corresponding libidinal economy, onto the Greece of Sophocles. That Freud could theorize the bourgeois nuclear family on the basis of a play from the fifth century B.C.E., or that Thomas Aquinas and William of Ockham could, in the late Middle Ages, draw on Aristotle to lay some of the foundations of modern bourgeois thought, has always seemed to me to present Marxist historiography with a potential problem. A possible solution was implicitly suggested by the work of Nietzsche, Spengler, and Heidegger (and directly suggested by Adorno and Foucault)—namely that social evolution in Ancient Greece must have anticipated in a number of ways that of modernity for Greece to have been able to retain its amazingly constant function as a source of inspiration to the West. But one would like to see a more direct economic link established. Thus, for example (and this

example is of direct and crucial relevance to the nexus of the existentialist problematic of the absurd and the rise of a market economy in modernity which we examined in relation to *Nausea*), it has always seemed to me that if there is an uncanny similarity between the evolution of the treatment of "being" (in Parmenides), universals (general concepts—"ideas" or "forms" in Plato), and particular or individual things from Parmenides through Plato to Aristotle in the classical period, and the sudden eclipse of Augustinian Platonism by Aristotelian Thomism and nominalism in the Middle Ages, it is because both social formations were struggling to comprehend and manage the new realities forced upon them by the increasing presence of *money* (an abstract universal equivalent having only exchange-value and no use-value) in economies previously based on barter (the exchange of particular things having use-value in daily life—still true of an early universal equivalent, cattle in Homer for example).

With regard to our case in point (Oedipus etc.), I speculate that the passage from earlier forms of the manorial household of the landed gentry than that on which the final version of the epic would be based (that of Odysseus, for example—already, it must be said, bearing little trace of an extended kin group) to the palace of the city-state (that of Creon or Oedipus) must have entailed a progressive constriction of the extended family culminating in something closer to the modern nuclear family. Which is what makes for the sudden topicality of what Freud would later call the Oedipus complex in Sophocles' massive elaboration of what had only been a passing reference to the myth of Oedipus in Homer. Hegel pointed out, in a number of passages of the *Aesthetic*, the conflict between the family and the nascent state in the Greek drama (most especially in *Antigone*); and we have seen how the *Oresteia* evokes the supplanting of the family by the state as the embodiment of the law. Both these examples suggest that an extended family is being replaced by a nuclear one (this is indeed what a state ideally requires—small units of social organization rather than large aggregates like clans [or feudal sub-conglomerates—witness the difficulty the absolute monarchy experienced in Europe in the face of the feudal nobility] which may defy or threaten the state). I am grateful to Keith Dickson for bringing to my attention the important reforms of Cleisthenes at the end of the sixth century B.C.E. which were intended to curtail the power of a handful of aristocratic extended familial clans by dividing Attica into *demes* based on topography. Thus instead of being named so-and-so, son of so-and-so of a particular clan, citizens still retained the patronymic but dropped the clan name in favor of the name of the *deme* to which they belonged. Dickson also tells me that from the beginning of the sixth century there is a significant decline in the relative freedom women had enjoyed (they are increasingly confined to the house) and a rise in misogyny in the literature of the later period. Thus the nexus of Oedipus, a nuclear family of sorts, misogyny, and a governing state taking precedence over groupings based on kinship is common to both the classical period and modernity. It is not for nothing that the intensely misogynistic and anti-natural *Nausea* is contemporaneous with the rise of fascism and a related simultaneous demotion of nature/woman (as in *Nausea* the two are assimilated to each other) which was denounced at the time (1944) by Theodor Adorno and Max Horkheimer: "Nature, on the other hand, is seen as something outside practical life and at a lower level, like the soldiers moll in the popular mind"—*Dialetic of Enlightenment,* trans. John Cumming (London: Verso, 1979), p.252. It is only logical, therefore, for Sartre to turn to a classical model like Aeschylus—a figure at the beginning of the tradition at the end of which Sartre finds himself, and whose play he will hijack for his own ends—for his attempted (and finally problematical—see note 5) overthrow of Oedipus, patriarchy, the nuclear family, and the modern state.

7. *The Iliad of Homer,* trans. Richmond Lattimore (Chicago: University of Chicago Press, 1961) 62.

8. Sigmund Freud, "Analysis Terminable and Interminable," *Therapy and Technique,* ed. Philip Rieff (New York: Macmillan, 1963) 268ff.

9. *Sartre on Theater* 226ff.

10. Also published in English as *Loser Wins.*

11. The entire plot is deliberately set in motion and controlled by the father from start to finish. His single motive from the outset is to get Frantz to come down from his room so that he may see him before dying, and in order to persuade his son to commit suicide with him. He puts Johanna and Werner on the spot (obliging Werner to swear to remain in the house) in order to provoke Johanna into trying to get to see Frantz so that she can gain their freedom by persuading him to come down. When this fails because Frantz suc-

ceeds in luring her into a pact of mutual delusion—she will believe his verson of the events of 1944 if he will find her truly beautiful, thus prolonging Frantz's sequestration in his room—when this fails, the father tells Leni that Johanna has been seeing Frantz. As the father had hoped, Leni, who is in love with her brother, deliberately tells Johanna, in front of Frantz, the truth of the events of 1944 on the Eastern Front in order to drive them apart. Frantz does indeed immediately lose all interest in Johanna (a reaction she recipro-cates), and is now able to face his father (because someone other than Leni now knows the horrifying truth) and leaves his room.

12. The decline in Sartre's reputation is frequently attributed to the discrediting of Marxism by association with the manifestly op-pressive political situation in the Soviet Union and Russian imperi-alism abroad. This is not really convincing, however, for reasons already cited earlier (Western leftists had consistently distinguished Marxism from Soviet communism); but one would want to point in addition to the fact that the Marxist Althusser would wield enor-mous influence in intellectual circles in Paris in the sixties well after Sartre had been declared *passé*. Sartre's eclipse (and the eventual disappearance of Marxism itself from the French intellectual scene) is more fundamentally related to the processes of social change ex-amined here. For a more extended account of these processes, see my forthcoming *From Existentialism to Poststructuralism and the Coming of the Postindustrial Age* (Stanford University Press). Fi-nally, some mention should be made of the fact that Sartre's relation-ship with Marxism was a difficult one. He consistently refused to join the French Communist Party and his relations with the latter oscil-lated from wary mutual support to violent mutual hostility. At the time of writing he maintained that his *Critique of Dialectical Rea-son* sought to renovate Marxism from within by means of the incor-poration of existentialism, with the latter nonetheless subordinate to the former. In late interviews, when he was no longer writing, he would reverse what he saw to be the relations between Marxism and existentialism in his work, giving priority to his existentialist notion of freedom. On the whole, I see no reason, however, not to describe Sartre as a Marxist (the question is sometimes controversial). He continued to the end to subscribe to the theory of surplus value, to the notions of class-struggle and the eventual triumph of socialism. If one is not to define Sartre as a Marxist, then one is going to have

to exclude other no less eccentric Western Marxist figures like Walter Benjamin or Ernest Bloch.

13. Sartre, *Situations II* (Paris: Gallimard, 1948) 316; my translation.

BIBLIOGRAPHY

Works by Sartre

Sartre's bibliography is overwhelming in its length, and the following compilation is by no means exhaustive. For works prior to 1970 the definitive text is Michel Contat and Michel Rybalka, *Les Ecrits de Sartre* (Paris: Gallimard, 1970). There exists an English translation by Richard C. McCleary which has been updated through 1974, *The Writings of Jean-Paul Sartre*, vol. 1, *A Bibliographical Life*, and vol. 2, *Selected Prose* (Evanston: Northwestern University Press, 1974). For the original French texts listed below, the place of publication is Paris and the publisher is Gallimard unless otherwise indicated.

La Transcendance de l'Ego, esquisse d'une description phénoménologique. First published in *Recherches philosophiques* 1936; reprinted in edition by Sylvie le Bon, Vrin, 1965. [*The Transcendence of the Ego.* Trans. Forrest Williams and Robert Kirkpatrick. New York: Noonday Press, 1957.]

L'Imagination. Alcan, 1936. [*Imagination: A Psychological Critique.* Trans. Forrest Williams. Ann Arbor: University of Michigan Press, 1962.]

La Nausée, 1938. [*Nausea.* Trans. Lloyd Alexander. New York: New Directions, 1964.]

Le Mur, 1939. [*The Wall.* Trans. Lloyd Alexander. New York: New Directions, 1975.] In addition to the title story this contains "The Room," "Erostratus," "Intimacy," and "The Childhood of a Leader."

Esquisse d'une théorie des émotions. Paris: Hermann, 1939. [*The Emotions: Outline of a Theory.* Trans. Bernard Frechtman. New York: Philosophical Library, 1948.]

BIBLIOGRAPHY

*L'Imaginaire, Psychologie phénoménologique de l'imagina-
tion*, 1940. [*The Psychology of Imagination*. Trans. Bernard
Frechtman. New York: Washington Square Press, 1968.]

Les Mouches, 1943. [*The Flies*. Trans. Stuart Gilbert. *No Exit
and Three Other Plays by Jean-Paul Sartre*. New York:
Vintage Books, 1955.]

L'Etre et le Néant, Essai d'ontologie phénoménologique, 1943.
[*Being and Nothingness: An Essay on Phenomenological
Ontology*. Trans. Hazel Barnes. New York: Philosophical
Library, 1956.]

Huis clos, 1945. [*No Exit*. Trans. Stuart Gilbert. *No Exit and
Three Other Plays by Jean-Paul Sartre*. New York: Vintage Books, 1955.]

L'Age de raison, 1945. [*The Age of Reason*. Trans. Eric Sutton. New York: Vintage Books, 1973.]

Le Sursis, 1945. [*The Reprieve*. Trans. Eric Sutton. New
York: Vintage Books, 1973.]

L'Existentialisme est un humanisme. Paris: Nagel, 1946.
["Existentialism Is a Humanism." Trans. Philip Mairet.
In *Existentialism from Dostoevsky to Sartre*. Ed. Walter
Kaufmann. New York: Meridian Books, 1957.]

Morts sans sépulture. Lausanne: Marguerat, 1946. [*The Vic-
tors*. Trans. Lionel Abel. New York: Knopf, 1949.]

La Putain respectueuse. Paris: Nagel, 1946. ["The Respectful
Prostitute." Trans. Lionel Abel. *No Exit and Three Other
Plays by Jean-Paul Sartre*. New York: Vintage Books,
1955.]

Réflexions sur la question juive. P. Morihien, 1946. [*Anti-
Semite and Jew*. Trans. George T. Becker. New York:
Schocken, 1948.]

Les Jeux sont faits. Paris: Nagel, 1946. [*The Chips Are Down*.
Trans. Louise Varèse. New York: Lear,1948.]

Situations I–X, 1947–1976. Substantial portions of these ten
volumes of literary, political, philosophical, and autobiographical essays and interviews have been published in
English in the following works:

What Is Literature? Trans. Bernard Frechtman. New York: Washington Square Press, 1966.

Literary and Philosophical Essays. Trans. Annette Michelson. New York: Collier Books, 1967.

Literary Essays. Trans. Annette Michelson. New York: Citadel, 1978.

Essays in Aesthetics. Trans. Wade Baskin. New York: P. Owen, 1963.

Situations. Trans. Benita Eisler. New York: Braziller, 1965.

The Communists and Peace. Trans. Martha Fletcher et al. New York: Braziller, 1968.

The Ghost of Stalin. Trans. Martha Fletcher. New York: Braziller, 1968.

Politics and Literature. Trans. J. A. Underwood and John Calder. London: Calder and Boyars, 1973.

Between Existentialism and Marxism. Trans. John Mathews. New York: Morrow, 1974.

Sartre on Theater. Trans. Frank Jellinek. New York: Random House, 1976.

Baudelaire, 1947. [*Baudelaire.* Trans. Martin Turnell. New York: New Directions, 1950.]

Les Mains sales, 1948. [*Dirty Hands.* Trans. Lionel Abel. *No Exit and Three Other Plays by Jean-Paul Sartre.* New York: Vintage Books, 1955.]

L'Engrenage. Paris: Nagel, 1948. [*In the Mesh.* Trans. Mervyn Savill. London: Dakers, 1954.]

La Mort dans l'âme, 1949. [*Troubled Sleep.* Trans. Gerard Hopkins. New York: Vintage Books, 1951. Published in London as *Death in the Soul.*]

Le Diable et le Bon Dieu, 1951. [*The Devil and the Good Lord.* Trans. Kitty Black. New York: Knopf, 1960.]

Saint Genet, comédien et martyr, 1952. [*Saint Genet, Actor and Martyr.* Trans. Bernard Frechtman. New York: Braziller, 1963.]

Kean, 1954. [*Kean.* Trans. Kitty Black. London: H. Hamilton, 1954.]

Nékrassov, 1956. [*Nekrassov.* Trans. Sylvia and George Leeson. London: H. Hamilton, 1956.]

Les Séquestrés d'Altona, 1960. [*The Condemned of Altona.* Trans. Sylvia and George Leeson. New York: Knopf, 1961.]

Critique de la raison dialectique, précédé de Questions de Méthode, I, Théorie des ensembles pratiques, 1960. [*Critique of Dialectical Reason.* Trans. Alan Sheridan-Smith. London: New Left Books, 1976.] The essay which precedes the main text (*Questions de méthode*) has been published separately as *Search for a Method,* trans. Hazel E. Barnes (New York: Knopf, 1963).

Les Mots, 1963. [*The Words.* Trans. Bernard Frechtman. New York: Fawcett, 1966.]

Les Troyennes (Euridipe, Les Troyennes, adaptation française de J.-P. Sartre), 1965. [*The Trojan Women.* Trans. Ronald Duncan. New York: Knopf, 1967.]

l'Idiot de la famille, Gustave Flaubert de 1821 à 1857, vols. 1 and 2, 1971; vol. 3, 1972. [*The Family Idiot.* Vols. 1 and 2. Trans. Carol Cosman. Chicago: University of Chicago Press, 1981, 1987.] There exists a revised and corrected French edition (Gallimard, 1988) which contains Sartre's notes for the incomplete fourth volume in an appendix to the third volume.

On a raison de se révolter (One is Right to Revolt), 1974. Discussions with Philippe Gavi and Pierre Victor.)

Sartre, 1977. Text of film "Sartre par lui-même." [*Sartre by Himself.* Trans. Richard Seaver. New York: Urizen Books, 1978.]

Oeuvres romanesques. Ed. Michel Contat and Michel Rybalka, 1981.

Les Carnets de la drôle de guerre, 1983. [*War Diaries: Notebooks from a Phony War, 1939–1940.* Trans. Quintin Hoare. London: Verso, 1984.]

Lettres au Castor et à quelques autres (Letters to the Beaver and a Few Others), 1983.

Cahiers pour une morale (Notebooks for an Ethic), 1983.

Mallarmé: la lucidité et sa face d'ombre. Ed. Arlette Elkaïm-Sartre. 1986. [*Mallarmé: Or, the Poet of Nothingness.* Trans. Ernest Sturm. University Park. Pennsylvania State University Press, 1987.]

Le Scénario Freud, 1984. [*The Freud Scenario.* Trans. Quintin Hoare. Chicago: University of Chicago Press, 1986.]

Critique de la raison dialectique, vol. 2 (inachevé), L'Intelligibilité de l'histoire (*Critique of Dialectical Reason, vol. 2 (incomplete), The Intelligibility of History*). Ed. Arlette Elkaïm-Sartre. 1985.

Critical Works

The volume of secondary material on Sartre is immense. The following selection constitutes suggestions as to the most helpful and representative works.

Bibliographies

Alden, Douglas W., and Richard A. Brooks. *A Critical Bibliography of French Literature,* vol. 6: *The Twentieth Century,* 3 vols. Syracuse: Syracuse University Press, 1980.

Lapointe, François, and Claire Lapointe. *Jean-Paul Sartre and His Critics: An International Bibliography (1938–1975).* Bowling Green, OH. Philosophy Documentation Center, 1975.

Lapointe, François L. "A Selective Bibliography with Notations on Sartre's *Nausea* (1938–1980)." Supplement to *Philosophy Today* 24 (Fall 1980): 285–96. Annotated.

———, and Claire Lapointe. "A Bibliography of Jean-Paul Sartre, 1970–1975: The Anglo-American Response to Jean-

Paul Sartre." *Philosophy Today* 19, (Winter 1975): 341–57. Lists books, doctoral dissertations and articles by topic.

Wilcocks, Robert. *Jean-Paul Sartre: A Bibliography of International Criticism.* Edmonton: University of Alberta Press, 1975.

Books

Aronson, Ronald. *Jean-Paul Sartre: Philosophy in the World.* London: New Left Books, 1980. Helpful overview of the major phases in Sartre's work.

———. *Sartre's Second Critique.* Chicago: University of Chicago Press, 1987. Useful commentary on the posthumously published second volume of *Critique of Dialectical Reason.* Makes an important contribution in pointing to the *Critique*'s origins in an attempt to defend Marxism against the criticisms formulated by Merleau-Ponty.

Autour de Jean-Paul Sartre: Littérature et philosophie. Introduction by Pierre Verstraeten. Paris: Gallimard, 1982. Colloquium. Excellent papers followed by animated discussions of high quality. Focuses primarily on Sartre's greatest work, the biographical study of Flaubert, *The Family Idiot.*

Beauvoir, Simone de. *Les Mémoirs d'une jeune fille bien rangée.* Paris: Gallimard, 1958. [*Memoirs of a Dutiful Daughter.* Trans. James Kirkup. New York: Harper, 1974.] Autobiographical account of de Beauvoir's youth and the beginning of her lifelong relationship with Sartre in their student days.

———. *La Force de l'Age.* Paris: Gallimard, 1960. [*The Prime of Life.* Trans. Peter Green. New York: World, 1962.] Autobiographical account of de Beauvoir's and Sartre's lives in the 1930s and the Second World War.

———. *La Force des choses.* Paris: Gallimard. 1963. [*The Force of Circumstance.* Trans. Richard Howard. New York:

Putnams, 1964.] De Beauvoir's and Sartre's lives from the Liberation to the early 60a.

———. *Tout compte fait*. Paris: Gallimard, 1972. [*All Said and Done*. Trans. Patrick O'Brien. New York: Putnam, 1974.] De Beauvoir's and Sartre's lives from 1962 to the early 70s.

———. *La Cérémonie des adieux, suivi de Entretiens avec Jean-Paul Sartre*. Paris: Gallimard, 1981. Recounts the last ten years of their life together. A grim and brutally frank account of Sartre's slow decline and death. Highly personal interviews with Sartre.

These volumes, with Sartre's autobiographical *Words,* have been the most important sources for information about Sartre's life. Their essentially positive portrayal of Sartre, de Beauvoir's life with Sartre, and his influence on her own literary career are convincingly problematized by Suzanne Lilar (see below).

Burnier, Michel-Antoine. *Choice of Action: The French Existentialists on the Political Front Line*. Trans B. Murchland. New York: Random House, 1968. Useful account of the evolution, over some twenty years, of the political positions and activities of Sartre and Merleau-Ponty.

Catalano, Joseph S. *A Commentary on Jean-Paul's "Being and Nothingness."* New York: Harper, 1974. Very helpful.

———. *A Commentary on Jean-Paul Sartre's "Critique of Dialectical Reason": Vol. 1, Theory of Practical Ensembles*. Chicago: University of Chicago Press, 1986. Very helpful.

Caws, Peter. *Sartre*. London: Routledge and Kegan Paul, 1979. Good overview of the philosophical works.

Cohen-Solal, Annie. *Sartre 1905–1980*. Paris: Gallimard, 1985. [*Sartre: A Life*. Trans. Anna Cancogni. New York: Pantheon, 1987.] The most copiously documented and researched biography to date.

Collins, Douglas. *Sartre as Biographer*. Cambridge: Harvard University Press, 1980. An excellent introduction to the biographies of Baudelaire, Genet, and Flaubert.

Danto, Arthur. *Jean-Paul Sartre.* New York: Viking, 1975. Slim, elegant, and accessible account of the early philosophy (*Being and Nothingness*).

Goldthorpe, Rhiannon. *Sartre: Literature and Theory.* Cambridge: Cambridge University Press, 1984. Contains a very useful discussion, in the final chapter, of Sartre's notion of committed literature.

Gorz, André. *Fondements pour une morale.* Paris: Galilée, 1977. An attempt by a close friend and collaborator to produce the existentialist ethic Sartre had promised at the end of *Being and Nothingness* and never provided. A remarkable work, easily on a par with anything Sartre ever wrote. Throws important light on *Being and Nothingness*.

Hayman, Ronald. *Writing Against: A Biography of Sartre.* London: Wiedenfeld and Nicolson, 1986. Gossipy; and occasionally gives way to facile malice, and so has to be read with vigilance. But draws together abundant information dispersed in other texts.

Hollier, Denis. *Politique de la prose: Sartre et l'année quarante.* Paris: Gallimard. 1982. [*The Politics of Prose: Essay on Sartre.* Trans. Jeffrey Mehlman. Foreword Jean-François Lyotard. Minneapolis: University of Minnesota Press, 1986.] Skillful, ultimately hostile, analysis inspired by post-Sartrean French philosophy. With the foreword by Jean-François Lyotard to the English translation, very representative of recent majority opinion in Paris on the subject of Sartre.

Howells, Christina. *Sartre's Theory of Literature.* London: Modern Humanities Research Association, 1979.

———. *Sartre: The Necessity of Freedom.* Cambridge: Cambridge University Press, 1988. Excellent overview of Sartre's work.

Issacharoff, Michael, and Jean-Claude Vilquin, eds. *Sartre et la mise en signe.* Lexington, KY: French Forum Monographs, 1982. Esssays by Geneviève Idt and Serge Doubrovsky especially useful for any investigation of Sartre's sexuality.

Jameson, Fredric. *Marxism and Form*. Princeton: Princeton University Press, 1971. Chapter 4 is devoted to Sartre. Probably the best account of Sartrean Marxism.

———. *Sartre: The Origins of a Style*. 2nd ed. New York: Columbia University Press, 1984. The second edition contains an important afterword by this leading Marxist critic.

Jeanson, Francis. *Sartre dans sa vie*. Paris: Seuil, 1974. A good biography, by a friend and collaborator, written from a Sartrean existentialist point of view. Verges, however, on hagiography.

———. *Sartre and the Problem of Morality*. Trans. Robert V. Stone. Bloomington: Indiana University Press, 1980. Sartre declared this to be the only work which had ever taught him anything about his own work (perhaps cause for some caution).

LaCapra, Dominick. *A Preface to Sartre*. Ithaca: Cornell University Press, 1978. A useful example of a reading inspired by post-Sartrean French philosophy (primarily Derrida). Hostile. The author appears to have mitigated this reaction in more recent work.

Lilar, Suzanne. *A propos de Sartre et de l'amour*. Paris: Editions Bernard Grasset, 1967. Vehemently critical of Sartre's depiction of women and gender. Often to the point. Fails to recognize, however, that scenes of great ugliness and degradation (or sexism, generally) are not necessarily always endorsed by Sartre and, indeed, often serve a critical purpose within an aesthetic whole (see her treatment of "Erostrate" as one extreme case of this tendency).

———. *Le Malentendu du deuxième sexe*. Paris: P.U.F., 1967. An interesting, and important, corrective to de Beauvoir's probably overly positive account of her relations with Sartre.

Mészáros, István. *The Work of Sartre*. Vol. 1: *Search for Freedom*. Atlantic Highlands, NJ: Humanities Press, 1980. Good overview, especially of the early period.

Pacaly, Josette. *Sartre au miroir: Une Lecture psychanalytique de ses écrits biographiques.* Paris: Klincksieck, 1980. Very skillful classical psychoanalysis of Sartre's own analyses of other figures. Refreshingly skeptical and irreverent.

Poster, Mark. *Existential Marxism in Postwar France.* Princeton: Princeton University Press, 1975. Important and very helpful intellectual history of the period.

————. *Sartre's Marxism.* London: Pluto Press, 1979. Useful introduction to, and commentary upon, Sartre's Marxist writings.

Sartre after Sartre. Yale French Studies 68. New Haven: Yale University Press, 1985.

Schilpp, Paul A., ed. *The Philosophy of Jean-Paul Sartre.* La Salle, IL: Open Court, 1981. Important collection of essays and a late interview with Sartre.

Silverman, Hugh, and Fredrick Elliston, eds.. *Jean-Paul Sartre: Contemporary Approaches to His Philosophy.* Pittsburgh: Duquesne University Press, 1980. Useful collection of essays and an important late interview.

Verstraeten, Pierre. *Violence et éthique, esquisse d'une critique de la morale dialectique à partir du théâtre politique de Sartre.* Paris: Gallimard, 1972. Probably the best reading of Sartre's plays available. Not for beginners.

Special Journal Issues

Obliques 18–19 (1979). Interviews and unpublished fragments.

Obliques 24–25, 1981. Sartre et les arts. Interviews and unpublished fragments.